LIVING IN

SAN MIGUEL

Living in San Miguel:

The Heart of the Matter

by

John Scherber

San Miguel Allende Books
San Miguel de Allende
Guanajuato, Mexico

ACKNOWLEDGMENTS

Any book starts as an idea, and by its completion becomes a joint effort.

Thanks to my wife, Kristine Scherber, for her editorial and critical help, for her gift of the title, and for the interior design of the print edition of this book.

Thanks to Chet Kozlowski for cover text editing.

Cover Design by Lander Rodriguez
Web Page Design by Julio Mendez

Many thanks to Yvonne Hayes for the use of Tom Dickson's *Day's End*, the painting that graces this cover.

Thanks to Tom Dickson for his vision of San Miguel that is so complimentary to my more literary view.

Thanks to my readers, who have asked repeatedly over the years, when is the sequel coming?

Thanks to all those who shared their stories with me: David Bossman, Antonieta Espinosa, Nathan Feuerberg, Nancy Howze, Judith Jenya, Mark Johaningsmeir, Jim Karger, Kelly Karger, Claudine Langan, Gordon Logan, William Martin, Dr. Roberto Maxwell, Raé Miller, Jim Newell, Anne Nicolai, Jim Priest, Bob Remak, Aarón Romo, Laurie Sandefer, Lisa Tyson Sandefer, Wendy Weber, and Lynn Weisberg.

ISBN:978-0-9906551-0-7

San Miguel Allende Books
San Miguel de Allende, GTO, México
www.sanmiguelallendebooks.com

Also by John Scherber

NONFICTION

San Miguel de Allende: A Place in the Heart
A Writer's Notebook: Everything I Wish Someone
Had Told Me When I Was Starting Out
Into the Heart of Mexico: Expatriates Find Themselves off the Beaten
Path

FICTION

The Devil's Workshop
Eden Lost
The Amarna Heresy

(The Murder in Mexico mystery series)

Twenty Centavos
The Fifth Codex
Brushwork
Daddy's Girl
Strike Zone
Vanishing Act
Jack and Jill
Identity Crisis
The Theft of the Virgin
The Book Doctor
The Predator
The Girl from Veracruz

(The Townshend Vampire Trilogy)

And Dark My Desire
And Darker My Wrath

Table of Contents

INTRODUCTION

Every Sunday is house tour day at the San Miguel de Allende Library. In its colorful past this building has been both a slaughterhouse and a convent, and now it houses both English and Spanish language book collections. It also has a theater, a restaurant, meeting rooms, and is home to our local newspaper, Atención. Adaptive reuse is a phrase people live by here. House tour visitors begin arriving in the courtyard at about 10:30 to buy their ticket to see three houses and gardens of expatriates who have settled in this town of 75,000 to make a new life here in a place unlike the one they left behind. At 11:00 AM a group of musicians in Spanish Renaissance costumes begins to play traditional Mexican melodies. The buses leave at 11:30 and 12:00.

Whether they come from Tacoma or Toronto, this is a crowd that is primed with curiosity about what it's like to live here. These are the people I write for, and they are full of questions. What makes this town the way it is? How does all this work? Is it safe to live here? I don't like to use the word magical, but some of them will see it that way. Why is San Miguel still a powerful draw for both expatriates and tourists, even when most of the American press has written off México, perhaps for its own biased reasons, unrelated to the diverse and accommodating reality of this wonderful country? The presence of the house tour crowd, in spite of this barrage of propaganda, is testimony to their courage and independent thinking. These visitors' modest contribution to the Library's upkeep buys them a close look at the lifestyle of Americans and Canadians who have pulled up their roots and left their home country, often with little or no regret.

The crowd will be fascinated by the detail of what they observe in these homes: the furniture, the fabrics, the folk art, the terraces and gardens, and especially the long panoramic views from the windows of the principal rooms that invite them to embrace the historic feeling of nearly five centuries of settlement since earliest colonial times.

A while back, the Library management invited me to take a table at each of these weekly gatherings and offer my books for sale. It was not so much an opportunity to sell great volumes of books, since many people are reluctant to carry things around with them on a tour like this. It was more a chance to talk with people, a meet and greet, as I think of it, an opportunity to listen to their questions and supply what answers I could. Connecting with potential readers is a way of life for any serious writer, and I was grateful for the opportunity.

In these conversations, the question I heard most often was this: "Do you live here?" The next was, "How long?"

"Seven years."

"Do you have anything back in the States?"
"Only the kids, and they like to come here more than we like to go back there."

Another common question that frequently followed was, "Do you feel safe here?" My response was generally, "Well, San Miguel de Allende is about as dangerous as Duluth, Minnesota on a Sunday afternoon in June. You can find trouble here if you look for it, but if you don't, it rarely comes looking for you."

Over the course of many weeks of interacting with the ebb and flow of house tour traffic in this courtyard I began to gain a sense of the wide range of what people wanted to know, but had found in the past no easy way to ask. Some had never visited México before and were amazed. Others had seen only the beach communities, and were surprised at the rich character of the surviving urban fabric from the colonial era. There were the usual questions about the nuts and bolts issues of immigration and the cost of living, but also queries related to personal interests they had. Was there a good golf course near San Miguel? Were there many writers here, or painters? Did they need to learn Spanish, and was there a good place to do that? How about schools, if they had children of that age. Was there an easy way to meet other expats? What do you do for health care? What do people do here to amuse themselves?

In short, how can I find out how the expat experience really works?

Wherever I go I have to be an observer. It's part of my job. Listening to these questions, and many others like them is what drove me to write this book. In addition to the specifics, I wanted to provide a sense of the texture and flavor of daily life as today's expat in the central part of México. It is written for the curious house tour member who has more questions than time as he or she is about to climb aboard the bus. It is written for that same person coming out of the last of those houses saying to herself, thinking of what she has just seen, "I only wish I had remembered to ask him about..."

It is also written for people who, whether casually or seriously, are thinking about what such a change would mean for their own lives, and whether San Miguel is a good destination for such a move. What kind of preparation would it take? What is it like on a personal basis? Why do some people manage it better than others? How can I keep myself from making a big mistake?

This book, then, is a tour in itself, not of the houses or gardens of San Miguel de Allende, but of the day-to-day experience of living there. It will not answer every question the reader might have, but it will certainly answer some they haven't thought of, some they could never think of without spending a lot of time there. Think of it as a solid base from which to launch a further investigation of the expat experience in this part of México.

Neither is it a guidebook. I have consciously omitted any comment, for example, on restaurants and lodging, or car rentals, because services like TripAdvisor do it on a basis that is as fresh as the latest traveler's review this morning.

Rather than include many lists, I have directed the reader to a few major links where they can be found. This book is more about the taste and flavor of living in San Miguel day to day, and not so much about the mechanics of the process, although you will find much practical information within these pages.

I have also not addressed important questions about immigration, since the laws have changed several times within my tenure in México, and are likely to again during the life of this book. Your best option is to contact the Mexican Consulate nearest to your home in the U.S. or Canada, and ask them what you need to do. The visa process for long term residence will typically start there. Regional offices like that will also have various interpretations of the current law that I can't anticipate in a book like this.

Now, let's get started on our tour.

CHAPTER 1

WHY SAN MIGUEL?

What is all this fuss about? It's true that San Miguel is a historic town, and a World Heritage site since 2008. Unlike nearby Guanajuato, the state capital and home to the largest silver mine in the world, the Valenciana, San Miguel has no silver. But it does have fresh springs, and that was its appeal in 1542, when it became a way station for the silver caravans on the way to Veracruz for shipment to Spain. With its other neighbor, Dolores Hidalgo, it played the role of Lexington and Concord for México as the region where the first shots were fired in the War of Independence, 1810-1821. It's the town where the nation of México was declared to be free and separate from Spain by a wealthy local clique who had no authority to do so, but it worked all the same because people were sufficiently open to the idea of a change to be ready to fight for it.

It has architectural controls that make it nearly impossible to remodel any exteriors in the historic center. If you took away the cars, much of it would look like 1750. It has a population of about eight to ten thousand expatriates (out of 75,000), Canadian and American, some of whom wander around wondering whether they're living in the real México or not. So what makes this town a good, even a stellar place to live in as a foreigner, an expat? To make it worthwhile to sell your house in Denver or Dover and wave goodbye to the grown kids (who don't understand what you're doing), and come down here and take a shot at learning Spanish? In short, to chance making a fool of yourself, which is the essence of risk.

There must be *something* about this place, and there is.

Not too long ago the magazine *Condé Nast Traveler* named San Miguel de Allende, México, winner of its annual reader poll to select the world's best city to live in.

Here is a reference, you can copy and paste it into your browser, as with all the others that will follow. http://www.cnn.com/2013/10/16/travel/cn-traveler-top-cities/

In the previous year the winner was Charleston, S. C., and Paris came in at #22. An impressive showing for this middling city in the central highlands of México, and perhaps a bit surprising considering the competition, but it does suggest that many people realize that San Miguel has some superior things to offer. I confess that my first reaction to this announcement was mild skepticism. This town has its warts, and I'm not sentimental about it. I like to enjoy it on its own merits, but I'm always aware of the bad as well as the good. If I had been asked, I would've said this was the best city I knew of that I could afford to live in, which is not so bad, although this is a criterion that Conde Nast's survey does not appear to offer. I suspect their target reader doesn't need to think much about it either.

While the magazine doesn't volunteer to share the reasons for its readers' rankings, it's easy to guess what some of them might be: a prodigious historic colonial charm, mostly intact and in some ways suggestive of Europe; a moderate and dependably sunny climate in most months, a low cost of living compared to the U.S. and Canada, the relative absence of heavy traffic, great cultural resources and restaurants, and an overall superior quality of life. Coming from Minnesota, I especially enjoy not having to even think about winter. If there is some aspect of that season I wish to explore, like the delicate crystalline structure of snowflakes, I can always find it on the National Geographic Channel. Somehow, I have never looked.

In short, these are the usual suspects when people start to think about where they might head next after deserting Newark or Detroit. I'm not going to argue with it, since I've lived in San Miguel myself for the better part of the last decade, and while I do occasionally long for Paris or Florence, those yearnings haven't yet prompted me to put my house on the market. San Miguel is a great place to be a writer, indeed, a creative person in any of the arts, and that's my niche. There is more about this, with some examples, in the chapter called CREATIVE LIVES.

One effect the Condé Nast piece did have was to prompt me to think about some reasons for this popularity that I knew were almost certainly not on that undisclosed list. Think of them as the insider's reasons to be here, because they don't all come into focus on your first, or even second, visit.

Number one I would call *Cultural Differences*. This town does not possess the seamless social fabric of central Iowa, and while it is small enough so that many people here know each other, and even more look familiar, it is still not a melting pot where everyone is merging into a smoothly blended culture. The Mexican community and the expat community both struggle a bit to understand each other's values and way of life. It is difficult to mistake members of one community for those of the other. In short, in passing, we always know which we are and where we belong. Still, it is easy to make erroneous assumptions about people who are different from us, and because it is a dynamic system, we all must work a little, and sometimes more than a little, to understand each other. If this keeps us slightly off balance, I see that as a good thing. It makes for sound muscle tone and mental agility as we get older, things that often tend to diminish in the absence of the challenge of change around us. Which brings us to the second point.

Number two would be *Respect for Elders*. San Miguel, like the rest of México, is not a place where being cutting edge equates with adopting this morning's newest trend. The calendar operates in fits and starts, and as a result, it is still 1950 in some areas here. We are not rushing to overtake the latest fad, so if you are not extremely young, you still have a chance of being at least somewhat engaged, since the values of those around you are not so fluid as to make yours seem rigidly irrelevant and old fashioned. We are more connected over the generations, and that feels good. Even people of advanced age are not segregated, and most families consist of very young children, parents, grandparents and great grandparents all spending time together to their mutual enrichment. In my childhood, I can remember it still being that way in the U.S., and I was privileged to know several of my relatives who had been born in the 1860s. Imagine growing to adulthood before the automobile was even invented.

Older people in México are generally regarded as retaining the wisdom of their accrued experience, and therefore deserving of respect. Solutions are often sought in the proven ways of the past. If they don't always work perfectly today, they may still be close enough, since the future offers even less certainty. In the hierarchical society that structures this country, age is an underpinning of the consistency of values, and a source of continuity both in attitude and in perceptions.

For the third reason, I would suggest what I call *The Carnival of Color*. While some businesses have branches and satellites, and we have nearby an Office Depot, a Starbuck's, and a Costco store in a neighboring town, this is still not in general a country hospitable to franchises or chains, although many Mexicans look on the big box stores as a sign of progress. As a result, you are likely to see behind the counter of your local bakery or dry cleaners the man or woman whose idea it was to start that business, a person who recognizes you and maintains his or her standard of product or service as a matter of pride, since commerce is still mostly seen as *personal*, a transaction that occurs within each other's space. When we buy goat cheese and yogurt at the organic market, we receive it from the hand of the woman who made it. I can think of many restaurants where the owner greets you at the door, and if he passes your table as you're eating, he says with emphasis, *buen provecho*!

While government-planned housing tracts (*infonavits*) exist on the edges of most large towns, and have a distressingly cookie-cutter feel, generally the housing stock is distinctly hand made and individual, using a robust variety of colors and materials. Our streets do not exhibit deadening parades of strip malls and franchise businesses, and the architecture is neither anonymous nor fortress-like in scale. We do not like to be mistaken for each other, and personal hospitality, based on recognition of friends and neighbors, is an established part of public behavior. The need each of us feels for uniqueness needs no justification. Exuberance is valued over reticence in design. It's OK to reproduce the Virgin of Guadalupe on the hood of your 1993 Dodge pickup. Subtle varieties of beige, however, are not easily distinguished this far south of the border, and I suspect are best appreciated against a backdrop of snow.

Number four I will call the *Mexican Dynamic*. For expats, it is impossible not to compare this country with the one we left, if only to reassure ourselves that we have given up easy access to chocolate chips and kosher dill pickles for sufficient reason.

The country of México, while older than both Canada and the U.S., is still tracing an upward curve in its economic development. The middle class is growing here, if from a smaller base, even as the middle class in the U.S. is shrinking. México is still creating jobs, since it dodged the worst effects of the recent recession in the States. While not a democracy in any true sense, its political life has been dominated by a single party for most of the last century. While this has fostered corruption and favoritism, more importantly, it has not constantly convulsed the country in political rancor and deadlock. Oddly, things can still be accomplished here at the federal government level.

People in this country do not take politics so seriously. There is a healthy cynicism about what happens in México City that Americans could examine more closely, since Mexicans are not as easily fooled by the nasty rant of self-seeking political parties on either side. This country functions more like Italy, where the government is simply not regarded as a serious player on the field of national life, a life that is more often sustained by the continuity of family and the tradition of the church, so the regime's periodic fall is often appropriately greeted with a yawn. The phrase I often hear in this country is, "Same horse, new rider." This is followed by a shrug.

Last comes number five, and it's my clear favorite. In terms of individual development, it's also the most important. San Miguel, and indeed México as a whole, is a place where expats can come and reinvent themselves, if that's their goal. Here, if you wish, you can have no history. Even if some expats don't see the process as one of reinvention, that's often what happens. Perhaps it's because we are obviously not part of the mainstream culture, and some (but not all) of those societal rules do not apply. For example, we are granted a pass from the class system here. This is an underlying theme I have written about before and will again. Moving here is a *Release into Freedom* at any age. It is a place with reduced or even absent expectations of what you might do or how you'll behave. It's as if your overseer has vanished, whether that was a family member, spouse, or a neighbor.

If you were a nun in your working life north of the border, you can be naughty down here without apologizing or blushing. If you were a plumber in Peoria, you can now be a photographer, a painter of portraits, or a poet. You can do nothing at all, or you can do *everything*. You can justify your prior life or simply forget it. The narrow, uneven sidewalk outside your door is labeled, in a script only you can see in a certain morning light, *Step One*. It calls out to you, inviting you to take charge of your life. Above all, you can unleash things from the subterranean layers of your mind, and as they emerge into daylight for the first time, you will need to apologize or explain them to *no one* in the entire world.

That is the charm of San Miguel and, indeed, of all of México.

CHAPTER 2

WHAT YOU THINK YOU NEED
vs.
What You Really Need.

There is no doubt that some things we feel we need are hard to find in San Miguel. One example is good bed linens, quality pillows, down comforters and duvet covers. Another would be high quality towels. If you're a runner, the availability of your very specific athletic shoe, your lucky footwear in six marathons, can also be a problem, as you study the steep slopes around you at 6,400 feet. Your precise choice of cosmetics may be available, but at prices that will make you blush. All these items can be had with some detailed searching, but why run around all over México, when if you are in the process of moving, you can simply bring them along? San Miguel is not a big city, and just as in the U.S., not everything is available in a town this size. You can order things to be brought down here by one of the mail services, but they will charge you for freight, plus 16% VAT, and you will likely pay the Texas sales tax as well, (because the delivery service has their pickup station there). Then you're going to pay México VAT on the Texas sales tax and freight charges as well, and it can get both irritating and pricy. I have found no good answer to this problem, and the best way to look at it is that it's a part of the cost of living and doing business here, which is amply balanced by the fact that your property tax will be $300 a year instead of $8,300, which was true in our case.

In addition, many companies will not understand why you are using Mexican information as you fill out their forms online, and they will reject it, as if you were attempting some scam. After all, aren't you an American? Haven't you read all the news reports about México? Most U.S. corporate computer systems were simply not set up to accommodate anyone living abroad.

Prescription meds can also be tricky. Often they are available here, but not always. If what you need is obscure or very recently developed, then you may want to bring a good supply with you (if you can), and that will give you time to analyze the supply situation on this end. You can also research the generic equivalents, which are popular here. And this will be a surprise: in México prescriptions are required only for narcotics and antibiotics. Everything else is freely available at the drugstore over the counter. Some of the services that bring mail and packages over the border for expats will not bring meds because of licensing and import issues, although that varies. If you are setting up an account with a mail service, check this issue before committing. Even if you don't need the meds now, you may later.

Under recent immigration law changes, you are not permitted to maintain a foreign plated car here if you have permanent resident status. Nor can many car makes be serviced in San Miguel by a dealer, but only informally, so if you have a recent Lexus or a Mercedes, or a similar import still under warranty, you might consider selling it before you arrive. If you come down on a temporary visa, once it changes to *permanente*, under the present rules, you will have only five days to take your car out of México for good. If you buy a car in San Miguel, you are assured of dealer service here. This is why we bought a Ford, after owning Infinitis and Saabs in the

States. Ford and Chevrolet, Nissan and Volkswagen are easily serviced here in town. For some, like Honda, you can obtain dealer service in nearby towns, like Celaya, for example, but do you want to drive an hour to leave your car with a dealer? Do you then wait all day in a rather charmless industrial town for an uncertain completion time to materialize? This is México, where times can be more approximate than in the U.S. or Canada. My limited experience with car dealer service is that it's more predictable than most other things, but even so, you can't always count on it.

Having a good experience living in San Miguel is about managing your irritants, and making your life easier with car service is one of the ways to do this.

In general, an effective strategy is to buy locally, and to learn the Mexican equivalents of your favorite products and use them whenever you can. You will pay far less for items that do not have to be imported, and their availability will usually be more predictable.

In a larger sense, isn't it fair to also say that you are not moving to México to replicate your former life? That was easier done by remaining in the place you just left. I have listed above a few specific examples, but let's look at a broader view. It's not just about regretfully walking away from your bittersweet chocolate chips or your favorite brand of Milwaukee kosher dill pickles. Here, to one degree or another, you will be walking away from many aspects of who you were up north, contacts and patterns that made up your daily routine. If you always watched *Wheel of Fortune* on television at six o'clock, you may still be able to do that here, but that won't be true of everything. Some people I talk to about the expat experience don't feel comfortable when I speak of it as reinventing ourselves, they reply that they see it as simply the next move in a series that is unbroken by questions of identity or transformation. That may be the case for many, and my own view may be colored by the fact that my writing career mostly developed after my arrival in México in 2007, so I might be tempted to see it as a bigger break with my past life than some others might with theirs. It is all a question of perspective and terminology. So, call it what you wish, but big changes are coming once you move. Anticipate what you can, and try to become flexible enough to accommodate those you can't.

Yet, aside from questions of reinvention or identity change, there is an issue of transition that comes from trading one living *context* for another, and that may not be clear until you arrive and settle in for a while, only to realize that you have altered more than your geography and your climate. You have changed the entire detail of your life. Some aspects may seem subtle, but the aggregate of all the detail that is overturned by moving to a different country is huge. If you were a cardiologist or an attorney, for example, at home, and you are now retired, you will find that the impressive social status you formerly had doesn't travel well. You will now be understood based on what you are doing since your arrival, in the new social matrix where you find yourself, unassociated with a hospital team or a group of your former law colleagues in a downtown high rise. Most expats will tell you that people you meet here will rarely ask what you did in your former life, because it was literally only that. It's no longer current. Will this be a drop in status? Possibly, but it is also an opportunity for growth. You have also lost some of your well-established status by having no power or connections in this community. You will in many ways remain an outsider, although the paleness of your skin (if you are white) will give you a certain lift socially, and there is also status to be had because as an American or Canadian, local people will consider you to be wealthy. They will address you as *señor.* Furthermore, they will wait for

23

you to greet them first, because that is your prerogative as a person of the moneyed classes.

If psychologically you need to retain the platform of your old social status, then this kind of move will not work well for you. This is where I see it as a reinvention, because much of who you were is connected with your old context, and that will now be lost. As expats, we need to find ways to redefine ourselves here, and to maintain a focus on the achievements of your prior life, while that may be the source of a rewarding reverie, may be perceived by others here as backward looking. Living in San Miguel is about starting a new life in a new place, and this process has many subtle nuances that only become apparent over time. Observing these changes as they develop will help you get settled and established sooner.

Similarly, those possessions associated with your former life won't have much meaning here. Your Mercedes would be a bad choice anyway in a sixteenth century town full of cobblestone streets and speed bumps, all to be endured in slow motion on the way to locate a too-tight parking place, where the cars ahead of and behind you are twenty years older than yours, which was made with the Autobahn and 240 KPH in mind.

These cobblestone streets were designed for burros. After all, don't forget that México is the home of the $80 car. Back in Cleveland, you may have thought that, after a lifetime of service, these decrepit vehicles all went to the junkyard heaven to be pressed into cubes and melted down. Certainly many did, but all the others are here, waiting in the shadows for you and your high-end BMW or Land Rover to appear, when they will suddenly lurch toward you out of a side street, as if the driver had no idea you existed. You find yourself suddenly covering your eyes to avoid flying glass, when you should be watching the road.

Your car also represents a display of wealth that's inappropriate in a country full of poor people, who, in an entire lifetime of hard labor, can never hope to earn the total of what it cost. The term net worth may often be heard in the banking precincts of México City, but in the parlance of the streets of any small town in the rest of this country it has no equivalent in daily speech. It is no secret why houses here are walled in, and the outside presentation of many of those walls is rather shabby to the eye. The stucco that drops onto the sidewalk may be swept up, but it is not always replaced. It's that we don't display even our modest wealth to the general public.

This raises a more general question: wealth? Well, it's partly about security, isn't it? We would not wish to one day find ourselves living on the *outside* of those nondescript walls that enclose our neocolonial mansions. That part makes complete sense. But how far does it go? A simple way to think of it is that there is no reason to buy things merely to express your status here, because that is not how it is expressed. We need to think of other, more creative ways, to do that.

Having and displaying great financial status may feel good, but it also makes you a target. Being here is not so much about who you are (or were, or what you have) but what you are doing in a phase of your life that will define you in many ways more than what you did before. We need to get ready for that. We will need to find things to do that make us feel good about ourselves and our community role without necessarily making extensive references to what went on in our past lives.

So, what do you *really* need in order to live a good life in San Miguel?

Without presuming to instruct you or read your mind, I would like to suggest that we, as prosperous expats coming down to San Miguel, need those things that make us comfortable in terms of housing, food, clothing, and a sense of belonging. Beyond that, we need what makes us happy and gives our lives meaning, but that will not be what once helped us compete with our suburban neighbors in the U.S. I had a neighbor there who spent in the upper five figures adding to his house only to make it look bigger: the interior space did not increase. We are not measured by the size of our egos here, although they do vary.

What I recommend is that we find something to get engaged with that we never did before, or if we once tried it, we reengage with it to a degree that was never possible in our past lives. For some, this may only mean relaxing in a way that our family or work commitments did not allow back in the U.S. or Canada. No excuse is needed to pursue that lifestyle. But I suspect that for many, it might be time to test ourselves a bit again. We did not come down here to be finished with our active lives, or because home nursing care is cheaper. If your first love in college was anthropology or archaeology, but you got an MBA in finance because it was more *practical*, then look around you. México is filled with ruins from a variety of eras and cultures. Our smallish state of Guanajuato has three pyramids that I know of, one within a half hour drive of where I sit writing this, even though it was never on the main axis of Mayan or Aztec civilization.

San Miguel hosts dozens of volunteer organizations, many of which would benefit from your experience and your lifetime of business insights. I know a man here who in his work life was dean of adjunct faculty at an Eastern college, who came down and became a bricklayer's assistant as he worked his way up to being head of one of these volunteer organizations, Casita Linda.

What is encouraged and even required here is thinking outside the box, because that box will be left behind you in a pile on the curb, waiting for the Good Will pickup in the town you came from. It was part of the vanishing context we looked at above. We will need to recall that taking risks can always cause us to stumble and look silly. Because I had always wanted to paint, I went to art school in my early fifties, working next to talented twenty-year olds. I resumed my writing career not long after. You have in your hands my twenty-first book. My house is hung with pictures I've painted, and dozens more of them were sold in Minnesota in the years before we came down here. One of my most well developed and valuable skills is getting up again when I fall down. I do have a few scars, but when I decide to do something, nothing gets in my way, especially myself and what I think my limitations might be now, or ever were in the past. Leave the fear and the ego at home. I can tell you for certain that it's more fun here without them. Nothing in Mexican culture will tell you what you cannot do in your creative life or in contributing to some worthy venture here; those prompts tend to come from within yourself. And yes, the local people will have more limitations than we do.

Open some doors that have been closed so long you don't notice them anymore when you walk past them in your mind. Then acknowledge that you closed them yourself, even though you may by now have forgotten when or why. Inside you will often discover surprises and opportunities. Dust them off and take a closer look. I once knew a woman who had wanted to paint for most of her life, but she told me that her husband had kept her from doing it. By then he had been dead for six years, but she still wasn't painting. The hand of the past is dead. It may be interesting to study, but don't let it dictate what you do in the present.

Awaiting their turn within you are all those things you never tried, or merely poked at just a bit, for whatever reason:

not enough time, family priorities, or your job occupied too much of your mind even when you were away from the office. You only wanted to relax, not work on something else. Of special appeal will be those interests that you set aside because, although they may have looked promising, they weren't *practical*. Let's also now set aside that term as a measure of any venture you might consider. We can better substitute *interesting* as a criterion for getting involved. Come here with enough money to live on comfortably, which doesn't need to be a fortune, and after that, forget *practical*. Think engagement, think now, think your future.

In my first book on the expat experience, *San Miguel de Allende: A Place in the Heart,* I began that series of conversations with the assumption that the key factor was the draw of this town itself—that it had an almost magical quality to change people's lives. By the end of that book I had proven to myself that it did not. My beginning assumption was simply wrong. In writing a book, it often takes over and shows the writer what it is really about.

What San Miguel *does* have, and this emerged so clearly as those stories evolved, is the quality of being the nearly ideal backdrop against which to play out the next phase of your life. As a receptive place for reinvention, for transformation, or for simply rewriting your life script in small but meaningful ways, it is without peer. I believe now, after my time here, that this is its perennial appeal, but it still requires your decision to make that happen. Some people come down here and bounce off this town, and return home to schedule their next México trip to the beach. That's all right, because this experience is not for everyone. Your task is to decide whether it's for you and the person you are with. There is no one else in this equation.

Wait, you are thinking, we only just applied for our visas last week. It's great that you've written twenty-one books, but you're kind of rushing me. I like my life pretty well here in Topeka, but it's only that, well, the property taxes get tougher every year, even though we've been in this same house since 1990. The last kid just left home in January at the age of twenty-eight, and she's only living with this guy, they're not married. We can hardly afford the cost of health insurance now that it's so much improved, and my old group policy—the one I'd had for sixteen years—was cancelled two months ago. Shop the exchange, they told me. Even though the Dow is high now, my 401K has tanked in this market. I used to think I could retire at sixty-five like my folks did, and their folks before them. I don't have any Spanish to speak of, even though, Karen, my wife, still speaks some high school French.

OK. The title of this chapter is *What You Think You Need vs. What You Really Need.* I think I can now answer this in one sentence.

To do this we need to restart ourselves, to reboot our operating system, an act that requires some energy and originality. To think of this transition not as merely an *experience,* but as the way your life will be once you have come and settled in. It is about living with a fresh challenge, with the willingness to change by degree. The first word on the list of the new and exciting skills you'll require is *patience,* both with yourself and those you will meet in this process. It is about not being done with your life, in all its permutations. It is more about being ready to open the dictionary to the words beginning with *re*: reconstruct, retool, reinvent, relocate, reimagine (a great one), reassess, rethink, relive, reconstruct.

Open your dictionary now, and turn to this *Re* page. The instructions are all there waiting for you. It says nothing about México in particular, and everything about how to jumpstart your coming life.

CHAPTER 3

CLIMATE AND WEATHER

Before choosing San Miguel we looked at a number of other Mexican cities. Although we knew we weren't headed for the beach, one place we especially liked was Mérida, about a half hour drive from the northern coast of the Yucatán. It was lively, with musical groups working the main plaza and some lesser ones, it had lovely architecture with a tropical flavor, and it was large enough, at around a million, to have all the services we would ever need. The housing was interesting and inexpensive. For $200,000 you could buy an utterly gorgeous house in well-maintained condition. It was nearly flat and filled with great walking streets. There were a number of fine restaurants. Some of the principal Mayan ruins are not far away. The problem was that the weather was hot and humid nearly all the time.

Coming from Minnesota, we don't pretend we are not climate refugees. Having never been skiers, Minnesota was a place we fervently wished to escape from five months a year, and if the warm weather turns out to be excessive in a different way, which it occasionally can, then you start the cycle all over again after missing the only good part. Mérida is also definitely a place you would wish to escape from a good part of the year. Neither of us likes to live in air conditioning. Regretfully, we crossed it off our list.

The perfect place to settle would be one with a climate that was at least livable and hopefully pleasant all year round. We don't mind traveling, in fact we enjoy it, but we don't want to be forced to do it, just to escape the weather where we live.

San Miguel is located in a shallow agricultural basin (the Bajio) at 6,400 feet in the mountainous center. It is on the latitude of Havana, so the altitude moderates the heat of the day by cooling off again at night. Each day begins at a cool temperature. It averages about fifteen inches of rainfall a year, most of it coming from June through September. Typically, but not always, during this period the rain arrives about three days a week and falls for an hour or so in the afternoon. This transforms the landscape. As in much of México, we have two seasons here: brown and green.

Typically the cooler weather occurs in November and December, lasting part way into January. If this period is sunny, which it usually is, then it's quite moderate, beginning in the low thirties to about forty in the morning, and rising to the upper seventies or eighty in mid afternoon. Most houses do not have heating other than gas units in unvented fireplaces. Before you start a wood fire on your hearth, make sure you have a flue to vent the smoke. Here is a key concept that will be fundamental to your comfort here: one of the most important aspects of designing or purchasing a house is considering its passive solar potential. Do *not* buy, rent, or build a dark house. This cannot be over emphasized, because the entry of the sun into the space you live in is your primary source of heat. Five of the seven winters I've spent here have been sunny, so the cool period is pleasant, if a little brisk in the morning.

Two of these winters had cloudy periods, sometimes lasting days. Nothing warms up. Without the sun, your morale droops and withers. This is as bad as it gets. If you're coming from Michigan this sounds doable, but remember—you have no central heating. However, the rest of the year never disappoints.

April and May are the warmest months, because after that, the rains come. I have seen the temperature reach 100° Fahrenheit, but the humidity has been around 10%, so I found it quite manageable. I don't know of any air conditioning here aside from in a few restaurants, but many homes have ceiling fans. When the sun is coming in too intensely through your solar-oriented windows, you pull the drapes.

I have seen only a single freezing night here within our courtyard. We lost a dozen leaves or so in our garden. Light frost occurs more often in the country, because here in town the heat absorbed in the masonry and pavement during the day radiates outward during the night. The mass of stone, brick and concrete in your house holds the warmth and stabilizes the temperature for extended periods.

Except for the fact that March tends to be a bit windy, that's about all there is to say about the weather. In fact, it would be possible to argue that, compared with places like Minnesota, San Miguel has no climate. The range of temperature here on the Fahrenheit scale that I've experienced is from 28° to 100°, a span of 72°. In Minnesota it went from 40° below zero to 105°, a range of 145°, twice as great. The principal difference day to day is whether the sun shines, and on average, on about nineteen out of twenty days it does a good part of the time.

Unlike some of México, San Miguel is not in the earthquake zone.

It is possible to live here without paying much attention to the weather, which suits me after too many years of harsh winters and thickly humid summers. There is no sense of hibernation, no changing of screens into storm windows and back, no checking the weather stripping, no raking of leaves or draining of hoses. No ice on the sidewalks. I once saw a bit of snow up in Santa Rosa, a town about seventy kilometers from here, but that's at 10,000 feet elevation.

Nor do we have tornados, which used to drive everyone into their basements in the Midwest in the late spring, or hurricanes. This is good, because we mostly don't have basements either.

México does offer a somewhat different cast of pests, however, and they have their own seasonal rhythm. The cockroaches are large, ranging up to an inch and a half long, but more typically an inch. They appear from the drains when the weather heats up in March. They are fleet of foot and harmless but for the filth that they carry. Ajax makes a floor-cleaning product called Expel that mostly keeps them out of the house. One or two a year will come in and keel over in some obvious place.

Scorpions are a different matter. Here they are small, sinister, slow, and usually brown. Expel has kept them out of the house but for two individuals over our time here. They are best addressed briskly with a men's shoe heel. They favor woodpiles, so handle your firewood with leather gloves on. Their sting is nasty to humans and animals, but not usually fatal. I have only seen two black widow spiders, one of which we killed at our kitchen door a few months ago. The other one was larger and I saw it near the front of my house as I was revising the final chapters of this book. They are shiny and feature a red hourglass on their abdomen. Their venom is fifteen times stronger than that of a rattlesnake, although a bite would not deliver nearly the same quantity. I understand that the tarantulas native to some parts of México are harmless, but I have never seen one here.

Mosquitoes are seasonal during the rains. They are

known to occasionally carry Dengue fever. The city will spray now and then, and we avoid keeping standing water in our fountains during the rainy season. They are fast and small, but never intense in my experience. You can certainly sit outside any time of the year and be only slightly bothered by them in summer, although they like some people more than others.

A friend discovered a rattlesnake in his garage, or rather his dog did, but he lives five miles out in the country. My sense of this part of México is that it seems like it ought to have more threatening fauna and vermin than it does, since frosts are both rare and light. It feels oddly benign to people like us, coming from a punishing climate, as if it can't quite be true. At first we sit outside waiting for the other shoe to drop, but this only lasts a couple of years, and then we relax and embrace the benign side of nature. It is easy to feel here that life is good.

As far as I can tell, the principal risk in this climate is that you can be gradually overtaken by a sense of solar entitlement. If there is a cloudy day, you may feel cheated. If there are two in a row, you could grow angry.

My best advice for people worried about the climate here is this: find a good hat, one made of straw that allows air to circulate through it, with a brim that overhangs your neck as well as your face. Naturally, there will be a large assortment to pick from. People sell them on the street, along with just about everything else. You don't need a roof here to do business.

CHAPTER 4

MONEY MATTERS

From knowing a little about México's economic history, I am aware of several unanticipated currency devaluations within living memory in this country's financial past, so I don't hold more than a thousand dollars worth of pesos at any time. Even without these official adjustments, this currency still endures a larger range of routine fluctuation than the American or Canadian dollar. In the time I've been here it's gone back and forth from 9.9 pesos to the U.S. dollar to 13.5, a spread of 36%, which can definitely affect an expat's cost of living. So if you are offered a deposit account interest rate here of 5% for one year, it may sound good compared with current low rates of return in the States, but scale that against a potential currency exchange fluctuation that can overwhelm your gains and quickly put your investment in a position of negative return.

Another aspect of this picture is that some deposit accounts are subject to taxation based on "high" balances, amounts that we would not consider substantial. If you are considering investing in a Mexican account, scrutinize these details carefully, since they change from time to time. The United States government is also interested in your foreign deposit accounts, and it pressures banks here (as elsewhere) to help them look over your shoulder. Until recently amounts above the equivalent of $10,000 U.S. required special reporting at tax time. These rules are also in flux so stay in touch with your tax preparer, bringing your funds down here and withdrawing cash on an as needed basis. I will have more about this in the paragraphs that follow.

My method of dealing with this is to keep my money in the United States, but that requires an easy and inexpensive way to bring some down here on a regular basis.

Like the chapter on public safety further on, I had already written this chapter once and placed it near the center of the book. Now as we rush to publication I've discarded it because, as sometimes happens, the contents have been rendered irrelevant by an act of Congress.

Two gentlemen in the Democratic leadership of the Senate attached a rider called FATCA to the budget bill, and effectively derailed the system used by more than ten million U.S. expats worldwide to routinely provide themselves with cash from their American checking accounts by writing checks abroad.

Formerly there were a number of places in San Miguel where, if you had an account with little, or even in some cases, no money in it, you could cash checks drawn on your U.S. bank. Many even offered excellent exchange rates. I once cashed a check for $3,500 on my account, which contained then about $20 worth of pesos. Life was simple and easy, a good fit for folks living south of the border. As I write this, the last financial institution in San Miguel cashing American checks has suspended this privilege.

At issue is the recent extension under FATCA provisions of financial reporting requirements to amounts as small as one centavo. The requirements, as I understand them, are framed in ways that do not reflect the record-keeping format of Mexican financial institutions and those of many other countries, so rather than jump through the hoops of reconfiguring their entire accounting system to comply, the banks are simply closing the accounts of Americans because compliance has become too expensive to consider. On the face of it, this Congressional measure gives new dimensions of meaning to the term *ill-advised*.

Was the point of this to identify those miscreants who were salting stacks of money away out of view of the IRS? If so, my suspicion is that most of those people were better prepared than the rest of us as a kind of fiscal chaos now rolls through the financial life of San Miguel's entire American expat colony, and in the rest of México too.

Of course, there is also the possibility that this intrusion into the harmless minutiae of our monetary life represents yet another extension of that insatiable lust for private information that seems to afflict people in Washington lately. My first choice would be to place a benign interpretation on this current overreach of constitutional authority. Was it only nothing more than sheer ineptitude, the inability to forecast even the most immediate outcome of this misguided piece of legislation—in this case ten million Americans world-wide scrambling to reorganize their financial existence on short notice. Like some other things, living abroad now seems to cause a frown on the Statue of *Liberty*.

So instead of providing a chapter with a set of detailed procedures for money management, as I had before, I am now left peering into a dirty wind, full of more uncertainty than what we normally have when dealing with a misguided bureaucracy, whether here or in the north.

If it does hold that no one will be able to cash checks here anymore, then we are confined in many cases to wire transfers or ATM cards. The objection to both is the expense. Most financial institutions charge $40 for a wire transfer. The free electronic funds transfers (ETF) that many Americans use at home cannot generally be used to make a deposit in a foreign bank. Whatever you use, you will then pay an exchange commission to move your funds from dollars to pesos.

Debit cards for ATMs typically charge a 3% foreign transaction fee. That can be a lot of money, and if you are paying that as you bring your income down for a month, that's $75 in just the *foreign* transaction fees, plus the basic transaction fees—perhaps eight times at $5.00 a time—each month to bring in $2,500. The cost will be $115, nearly 5%. For that money you could have an extravagant anniversary dinner for four, with premium wines and valet parking. To me that's a bit stiff, especially when these transfers used to be free just by cashing a check.

The task is clear. Go online and find a bank that will issue an ATM card that does not have a foreign transaction fee. Find a bank that will do wire transfers inexpensively. It is possible that some institutions will see an opportunity in this debacle and set up a way to make money by providing cost-effective solutions for American expats left stranded by their thoughtful Congress. There is a great spirit of entrepreneurship here and I wouldn't be surprised to see someone soon establish a niche business to fix this problem.

So why will you need all this cash, especially if getting hold of it has become a can of worms? Why not just charge everything?

First of all, most credit cards will also charge you the 3% foreign transaction fee. Furthermore, credit and debit cards here are not looked upon as favorably for purchases as in the U.S. or Canada. Certainly, if you are paying the bill in a restaurant, the staff will be very appreciative if you at least pay the tip in cash. The management will prefer to be paid that way too. Some people who withdraw money from their accounts at ATM machines have trouble periodically with the card number inexplicably being read, resulting in fraudulent transactions appearing on their accounts. Using your credit or debit card frequently places you at greater risk for this, so make sure your debit card has fraud protection, since not all of them do. If you're in the habit of charging a lot of transactions, then also check your balance frequently online, even daily. One advantage of getting cash via debit card withdrawals is that you may get the best exchange rate of all, even though that will not offset the foreign transaction fee, which can be a larger problem. Again, this may vary. Know your bank and your card issuer, and give your transactions much closer oversight than you would at home. Do the math to establish what your real costs are.

For paying utility bills or property taxes online, you will need a Mexican credit card.

The fact is that this is mostly a cash economy. Some of it is underground and flourishes there without paying the 16% VAT that the government levies on most visible transactions.

Checks are also looked upon with a jaundiced eye. You rarely receive them in payment, and few people will want to receive yours. Accepting a local one, taking it to the bank where the account of the issuer is, and trying to cash it can be difficult. Banks tend to scrutinize them with a magnifying glass, looking for the tiniest of errors. They will greet any excuse to turn it back to you, marked with nasty lines through the signature, with muted shouts of joy.

You will also be surprised at utility bills here. Some come in the mail, some come under your front door, but they never include a return envelope to mail back a check because they don't want one. On the reverse of the bill you will find a list of the banks or supermarkets where you can pay it in cash, *en efectivo* as it's called. You will need to go in person to the utility company office or one of these listed banks or stores and settle your account by the due date. Sometimes the electric company cannot even get you a bill by that due date, but you are still obligated to pay it on time or they will shut down your service. There are several reasons I have no chapter on the excellent customer service by utilities in this book, but chiefly it is because it would not occupy even a single paragraph, and I have a minimum standard as to what makes up a chapter.

Everybody who lives here knows these cash issues, so when someone is carefully eyeing your purse as you walk down the street, it is with the expectation that whatever business you are planning to do, you will be carrying sufficient cash to do it. Keep this in mind as you develop a strategy for physically holding on to your money. If you tend to loose cameras or purses in taxis, do not expect to see them again. Even if the driver is honest, which is usually but not always the case, the next passenger may not be.

Pocket change is an endangered species. The lack of it can be an excuse to charge you more than your bill, especially in taxis. Small amounts are generally rounded over, and not in your favor.

Trying to pay with paper dollars in restaurants or stores is the equivalent of wearing a large target on your shirt. After a few glasses of wine in a local bistro, your math skills may not be what they were when you walked in, and the management already knows that when they calculate an exchange rate better suited to Indian rupees than dollars.

Get a few pesos at the airport coming in, but not many (because of the poor rate), and then stop at one of the *cambio* (exchange) stations around the *jardín* (the central plaza) and cash a larger amount. Have your passport ready. Then pay in the local currency as you go dining or shopping. If you think about it, why should someone from the restaurant have to go exchange money for you? To not bother to obtain local currency might well be regarded as arrogant. Although dollars are appreciated for their fine engraving and top quality paper, they are not almighty here. Remember that historically, Mexicans have gotten the short end of the stick a number of times from Americans, once losing half their country for no clear reason (to them). So don't blame them for showing a bit of sensitivity, even this much farther down the road.

These are all nuts and bolts issues. At one time, as I was preparing to move down here, many of them were the questions that topped my list of concerns. I knew we had to have money ready right away, but how could we get at it without carrying down stacks of it? There are other answers, but these, at least, are methods that work as I write this. I encourage you to do your own research before you leave home and also when you settle in and find solutions that suit your needs and lifestyle better. It will mean you are catching on. The point of this book is to give you some shortcuts in that process. If it seems appropriate, discard them as you progress.

We all start out as greenhorns, and after my time in San Miguel, I still learn new things nearly every day. I am not a fan of gurus, and I don't present myself as one. I am more a fellow traveler in a very foreign place, offering a hand up to anyone thinking about what the day-to-day process of living here might be like.

I see tourists and newcomers on the streets every day, and they share a certain look. For one thing, the men are often wearing shorts, which most adult Mexicans and expats don't, and hats that might have come from a 1940s movie about the French Foreign Legion (L. L. Bean?). At intersections, they tend to point to a much-creased pocket map and scan the surrounding buildings with shaded eyes. I often stop and offer to help them. In their confusion and frustration, I can easily see myself as I was when we arrived. Even then, sketchy as my overview was, it was still a very good time indeed to settle in and explore this exciting experience of living in San Miguel. Talking to newcomers now easily connects me to those virgin times.

Here's a footnote that belongs to no place in particular, but here as well as anywhere: if you are requested to prove your address when making a transaction, they are asking for a recent electric bill. Make a photocopy and carry it in your wallet. Change it often enough so that it's approximately current.

I hope that by the time you read this, either the FATCA regulations will have been rationalized, or better ways of raising cash from American bank accounts will have been developed. I also sincerely hope that the center of this chapter will have become irrelevant.

If there is a lesson in all these changes it is that living abroad tends to keep you either nimble or confused.

CHAPTER 5

RETIREMENT COSTS

Setting up a scale of retirement costs in México is a popular activity on the Internet, but I'm not sure how useful it is except in a general way to compare one area of this country with another, based on the same assumptions. In a town of this size, one of the key issues is also whether you have an expat community present that is big enough to drive prices and availability. I typically tell people that San Miguel is one of the more costly places to live in México, somewhat on a par with the beach communities. But what does that mean in practical terms?

It starts with housing costs, and I've given some attention to that in the chapter titled HOUSES AND HOMES. In San Miguel, real estate, whether vacant land or finished homes, is clearly dominated by expat demand that varies in cycles from high to low. Go online and scan the offerings of some of the realty companies to get an idea of what your housing dollar will buy here. As in the U.S. and Canada, location within San Miguel plays a prominent role, along with whether people from the north are feeling wealthy or poor that year. People buying here for the first time often assume that it's best to be close to *centro*, the historic center that some might call downtown. How many blocks of level walking a house is to the *jardín*, the central plaza, is a number that is commonly cited. Because this idea is so widespread, buyers looking in that area will pay a premium for the privilege.

But is that where you want to be, or is it merely the too obvious and uninformed choice? Homeowners or renters in *centro* will also bear the brunt of the traffic during tourist season, which is about two-thirds of the year. What can be exhilarating on a Sunday afternoon at the end of your vacation visit often wears thin as it runs on outside in the street below your bedroom window at three in the morning.

If you are not a party animal, or a person with a need for nonstop stimulation, a better strategy might be to live out a bit in one of the quieter neighborhoods so that you can walk away from the fiesta when you've had enough. I can guarantee that many Mexican partiers can outlast you, even if you're from New Orleans and Mardi Gras is your favorite time of the year. It's also good to be able to simply drive unimpeded to the supermarket for your normal groceries, or to go for gas without being trapped behind or inside a parade or religious procession. You will not enjoy having the street barricaded two blocks away from your house and garage in every direction. Many Mexicans like to party long and hard as a release from all the backbreaking and poorly paid work they do, and the large numbers of fiestas here are embraced as an important way to blow off steam. As a person who may be a retired accountant after forty-four years of processing people's tax returns, you may well have lost the need to blow things out in a big way in your own life, so you will find you can get all of this you need and still have a good night's sleep if you live somewhere else in town.

Recognizing this aspect of reality will also get you a more reasonably priced house.

One feature of home ownership that will shock you is property taxes. When we left Minnesota in the summer of

2007 we owned a 5,000-square foot Cape Cod forty-three years old, in an upscale inner ring suburb of Minneapolis, and the property taxes were $8,300 a year. This is merely an example, and obviously, a number like this will vary widely all over the U.S. and Canada. Here in San Miguel we own a 4,000-square foot house, ten years old, and the taxes are $320 (U.S.) a year. Annual license plate charges on our seven-year old Ford Edge are about $27.00. We bought this car new here and it now has about 31,000 miles on it.

Let's look at monthly utilities. Gas for heating (the most minimal of all the uses), cooking, hot water, clothes dryer, etc., runs $24 a month on average. Telephone (landline) with Internet and a hundred minutes of cellular, is about $30 a month. Cable TV is $23. Water is $7.50, and electricity runs about $18.

A further word about electrical service. On your bi-monthly bill you will see three pricing brackets. The first tier of usage is quite inexpensive, the second tier higher, and the third is nearly four times the rate per kilowatt hour as the first. Obviously, this encourages conservation. If you use more than 500 kilowatt hours during this two-month period, you will be locked into this highest rate bracket for your entire consumption for the next six months, not a good place to be. If you buy or rent a house that has more than one meter, that's a good thing, because then you will get the same progressive rate structure for the area covered by each meter.

Besides turning out the lights, you can also obtain different lamps that have a lower rate of consumption. For example, we were operating seven fifty-watt spots in our kitchen, which is fairly large, and that meant 350 watts of consumption every time we turned the lights on. These were on tracks. We changed to Techno Lights, where a three-watt spot produces about the same amount of light as a conventional fifty-watt unit. Now, with six fixtures replacing the previous seven, we power the entire kitchen with eighteen watts of consumption. These are not the ugly bluish spiral lamps. They look very much like the previous spots, and the quality of light is just slightly different and easy to get used to. Six new fixtures cost less than a hundred dollars and the replacement bulbs are three times the cost of the others, but they last nine years. The effect of this change was instantaneous—our electric bill dropped sharply.

Pemex, the national chain of gas stations, is a monopoly owned by the Mexican government. The cost of fuel, although sometimes lower than in the U.S., does not differ greatly here.

This morning I paid three dollars for a haircut. Quality hair care for women, which is readily available, is much more expensive, but still not quite on a par with the U.S.

Our biggest expense is usually food. Here is where one person's costs will differ widely from those of another. If you buy large quantities of imported foods, or insist on American cuts of meat, your expenses will run much higher. Emphasizing domestic products, fresher but often less familiar, will save you money. It will pay to become knowledgeable about domestic equivalents. For example, I don't buy American cuts of beef here, or order them in restaurants. I find the local version inferior and overpriced. If they are said to be imported, that's not always dependable. Instead, look at *arrachera*, the local marinated skirt steak. Much less expensive, (and regarded as an inferior cut in the States) it's tender, flavorful, and great on the barbecue at about six minutes on a side. San Miguel has a number of fresh fish markets. Remember also that processing food here drives up the cost, as it does anywhere. Agribusiness in the U.S. is all about "value added." Today's Chicago wholesale price for a bushel of oats is $4.00–

–I checked it online. Convert that same quantity of oats into Cheerios or something frosted, and it's worth many times that. Dining in restaurants can vary widely in cost, but in general is much cheaper than in the U.S. Typically at 15%, tipping is the same. Mexican beer is generally of better quality and has more character than the mass-market brands in the U.S. Although I haven't tried many of the microbreweries yet, I suspect that since the basic brews are so good, their quality is high. Very respectable tequilas and mescal can be had for reasonable prices. For Azul, a high quality sipping tequila, we pay a little more than ten dollars a 750ml. bottle. You'll pay a premium for Scotch and English gin. Oddly, great buys can be had in French wines if you're not drinking the famous labels. Look for Barton & Gustier, a nearly 300-year-old French firm that blends vintage and non-vintage wines to create a product of remarkably dependable quality. You can buy in San Miguel their consistent and respectable Partager line for about eight dollars a bottle. This means they can buy the produce of small vineyards, blend and age it, bottle it, ship it across the ocean, pay the duty coming into México, pay the 16% VAT at the check out, and still make a profit. As they say here, "'Splain me," because I don't get it. Yet, I can easily live with it.

Buses are cheap at six pesos a trip ($.45) and cabs to most places in town cost thirty to thirty-five pesos. If you phone them to pick you up, expect to pay twice as much.

If you are sixty years old or more and have a *perman-ente* visa, you can get a government INAPAM card at no cost. It gives you free admission to most museums and archaeological sites, a discount on prescriptions at many pharmacies, and a number of other things that get added to their list periodically. Just ask at the check out. México has a superb intercity bus system, and several seats on each one are set aside at half price for people with INAPAM cards. Ask when you book the trip. For 500 pesos a year ($39.00) in San Miguel you can get a VIP card, a privately owned discount program that will give you discounts in restaurants and many other businesses, including the airport shuttle. The discount on my car insurance alone is worth several times the annual cost.

This book offers an entire chapter on health care, but in terms of cost alone in that area, let me add some issues here.

Our doctor, who is American trained and speaks perfect English, charged us 500 pesos for initial consultation and intake interview, which he did himself over the course of an hour. He gave us his cell phone number to reach him any time in an emergency. Should you have a heart attack or require emergency hospitalization you can call him and he will follow the ambulance to the hospital and get you admitted.

While healthcare is always one of life's major expenses, it is not an automatic disaster here, as it can be elsewhere. I know someone who fell on the sidewalk and spent a total of $60 for X-rays and a cast on a broken wrist. Some doctors make house calls at no great charge. We have had a number of healthcare issues, some including brief hospital visits—none overnight—and they have always been manageable—cured by a credit card. I have found no reason to think that the health care system in México is inferior to that in the U.S. My Canadian readers will have to use their own experience to evaluate this concept against cost and residency requirements. Certainly what we have here does not invite the attention of a legal profession that views medicine as its ticket to early retirement in Palm Springs. There is no equivalent tort system here. If your doctor connects your urinary catheter to the wrong tube and drains your brain fluid by mistake, that must be because it was fate. Get over it if you can. Seriously, what matters is that no one is ordering batteries of irrelevant tests here just to cover their ass so your lawyer doesn't sue them. People try their best (as they do in the States or Canada), and they're mostly damn good, but not always.

As I will talk about in the HEALTH CARE chapter, the United States Medicare system denies all claims originating from out of the country if you have been outside the borders for more than sixty days, even though you are required to pay the premiums no matter where you live, so that will be a decision to make when you decide how you wish to treat non-emergency problems. Health insurance policies are available for expats, and depending on the usual factors of age, medical history and deductibles, some that exclude treatment in the U. S. can be fairly reasonable. Air evacuation insurance is also available as an extra. As a precaution, check the current version of Obamacare, if you can. It is a program that changes by executive order rather than need.

So, the subject is retirement costs. Much of it is about how much you want to spend. How much do you have? How much do you wish to leave the kids? What was left to you by your family?

What do you need for staff? This can be a thorny issue, because, as I suggest in the chapter titled PUBLIC SAFETY, some of the crime issues here are directly connected to which people you will choose to regularly give access to your household. I don't say the idea is always bad by any means, and I know some expats who have listed their maids and gardeners in their will, but exercising caution and due diligence as to the household help is *always* a good idea.

Yes, you say, but my maid is trustworthy and nothing has ever been missing. She's been with me four years, now, and last year I gave her a key so she can clean when I go back to Houston to see my brother and his family.

Great, although three half days a week working for

you don't add up to any kind of a living for her. She also has to work one whole day at a dentist's office, and he always comes on to her when the last patient is gone. She's used to this, but even so, putting up with the harassment doesn't pay any better than just doing her cleaning job. What about her latest boyfriend, whom she met at the Tianguis (the Tuesday market) selling goods of uncertain provenance? When it comes to men, how can she ever be as selective as you are, when she has three kids with no male parent at home or even in view? This new guy is awfully nice, though, even if he's five years younger than she is. He doesn't bring that up, and he has taken a genuine interest in her job, which most men don't, stating that she must be really good at it to manage all of those tasks in a gringo household, where, as we all know, they can be so *demanding*. Are the ones you work for old, and do they ever take long trips out of town? Some friends of mine once returned from a trip and found their television set sitting out on the lawn.

The mercantile heartbeat of San Miguel is the Tuesday market, the Tianguis I mentioned above. You can find almost anything there. Certainly the fruits and vegetables are fresh and inexpensive, the chicken is cut up to order before your eyes, and the shrimp is fresh. You can pause for lunch before shopping for bootleg CDs and DVDs, and clothing new and used. Watch for discontinued patterns of fashions by famous label makers. I once bought a great new Tommy Bahama silk shirt for 120 pesos—less than ten dollars. I'm going to wear it to a book signing tomorrow night. This is today's version of the ancient traveling markets, setting up at dawn on Tuesdays and gone by nightfall, to reappear in the next town the next day. Does your dog feel a sudden hankering for chicken feet, or do you need a good used pipe wrench? No problem. This is the people's market, *par excellence*. It should not be missed.

San Miguel has several big box stores, and there are more, such as Costco and Home Depot, within an hour's drive in Celaya, a city of about three to four hundred thousand population south of here on a good highway.

In general, I think a couple in reasonable health could get by quite well on $2500 a month if they did not have rent or a house payment to deal with. This would not include special extras, like a large annual health insurance premium payment, a car purchase, extensive travel, large prescription costs, or other medical bills. I know of some that get by here on Social Security, although that would be easier in a town without a large expat population to drive the economy. I think of the cost of living as about half or slightly less than that in the U.S. From my research, I think there are also places further south that offer a better cost of living.

As you consider this, factor that into the increased quality of life, with the cultural resources, restaurants, and sophisticated shopping the presence of these Americans and Canadians supports.

CHAPTER 6

DRIVING

One question I was sometimes asked at the house tour was whether there were different rules for driving in México. Are there any rules? This country is to some degree a lawless land, and I'm not referring to the drug trade with the U.S. It's not that no laws have been put on the books, it's more that we as drivers need to know which ones, if any, are enforced, and when. That takes some getting used to, and it might be best approached with a bit of humor, which is how I'm going to handle it. Humor will help to reduce the anxiety the subject often has, and with a healthy dose of patience, will form the core of our principal driving attitude.

The truth is that the thought of driving in México strikes a deadly fear into the hearts of many Americans and Canadians alike. Of course, they purchased Mexican car insurance online before they crossed the border. Yet somehow this only made them feel legal, but not safe. Now here's the reality as they ease their $47,000 BMW onto the pavement and point it south.

They have heard that there is neither rhyme nor reason to the driving there, and worse, any clown can get a license. (Tens of millions of drivers don't even have one.) But they are tourists in the classical sense, and they plan to cruise from town to town and only stop when the spirit moves them.

Serendipity is a proven value in their lives, and they would never be caught taking a package tour, even to Antarctica. Furthermore, like everyone else, they hate what air travel has become.

Isn't that the dilemma for many travelers to Latin America?

Before my wife and I moved to San Miguel de Allende, she was driving a Saab and I drove an Infiniti. We knew they couldn't easily be serviced in this mountain town of 75,000, so we sold them and bought a Ford Edge when we arrived. There was the choice between a passenger vehicle and a pickup, and we had heard that license plates were much cheaper on new pickups, but we felt because of the limited passenger capacity, we had to choose the SUV. After all, wouldn't hundreds of our friends and family from the U.S. soon be flocking down to see us? We hadn't yet reckoned on the chilling effect of the crusading American media, obviously. After all, it hadn't stopped us.

Unfortunately, our estimate of any pickup's passenger capacity was wildly off too. We've since been keeping a running count on the record for the most passengers in a pickup. It presently stands at sixteen people and a dog. This can be very handy running back and forth to the countryside with your extended family, but it occasionally results in some astoundingly lethal highway accidents.

Since San Miguel is a great historic town, it appropriately possesses no traffic lights. Major intersections on the outskirts are handled by roundabouts, which are called *glorietas* here, as if navigating them successfully could ever be an elevating experience. The idea is quite simple, although it looks daunting to many. The circular center island is about a hundred feet across. In the middle is a monument to a patriotic figure, although some believe the statue represents Chaos, the god of traffic. Four streets converge at this circle.

Within, the traffic moves counterclockwise. You enter after yielding to traffic from the left, and continue around to the right until you exit on the first, second, or third street. Or you can go completely around when you're doubling back. If you can keep your wits about you it works well. People are generally polite and orderly. The worst move you can make is to freeze up, come to a complete stop trying to change lanes within the circle, and cover your face with your hands. I have seen this happen and it's never well received. People will start to nudge you along with their bumpers.

This town has a number of stop signs, none of them in the central part. They are all treated as advisory in nature, and I have never seen anyone stop for one unless the failure to do so would result in an immediate collision. This includes me.

All other intersections are handled on an alternating basis. You go, then I go, etc. Everyone understands this, and it works well unless the other car is being driven by a person from México City, Guadalajara, or one of the northern border states that is too near to gringo manners. In that case you are regarded as a fool and a victim for letting him through. This attitude will be well understood by people who regularly drive in the U.S.

Another common way of slowing traffic, and one that cannot be ignored, are the *topes*. Think of them as speed bumps. The come in all sizes. They will first of all determine whether your car was made in a place that has smooth roads with few obstructions, because if your clearance does not allow for a certain variety of *tope* height, you will find yourself looping back to search for your muffler, now strangely silent, although your car isn't.

Aside from this, in general there is an attitude of live and let live behind the wheel. I have not seen road rage here among Mexicans, only Americans. Indeed, people are tolerant of what I regard as free-style driving. A certain amount of improvisation is customary and widely accepted. If you see someone approaching head-on in your lane, the expected response is to change lanes yourself into oncoming traffic, which will then slow down to allow your eventual return to your own lane. The correct response to the near miss of a head-on collision is a casual wave to the other driver(s), acknowledging once again the great beneficence of fate.

The concept of speed limits is one that is mainly recalled from their training by the transit authorities, but is the object of crude humor among the general population, for whom driving is one of the great ways to showcase their machismo.

Flashing colored lights are widely appreciated on their own merits, but using them to signal turns when mounted on a moving vehicle is a concept that has not yet caught on in México. One exception is their use on trucks in highway settings. Say you are behind a double bottom semi signaling with its left blinker. This means one or more of the following: Pass me because it's clear ahead; or, I am going to turn left now; or, I turned on this lever by mistake and got a clicking noise and I'm not sure what that means. Your life depends on how you scan the nuance of this, but isn't that often the case in so many other situations?

In San Miguel the streets are generally constructed from the two most common compounds on earth: dirt, and stones about the size of a large grapefruit. The stones are simply set into a matrix of dirt. Over time, the dirt is pounded into a fine dry powder that floats upward and seeks the interior of your electronic equipment, where it settles once again in the tiny connections between the wires. Over time the cobblestones loosen and have to be repacked in more dirt, which is never in short supply. Driving over this rugged surface, charmingly suggestive of medieval London or Paris, gradually loosens all the nuts and bolts in your car until that new BMW sounds like a 1960s jug band as it lurches down the street.

Both tires and shock absorbers have the life expectancy of a butterfly in a hurricane. What the streets do not do to your car, the sun and weather will.

By now I hope I have established that what at first appears to be random and senseless is really a functional system that can be understood by most visitors with a knack for improvisation and a broad sense of humor. I should point out that I am writing mainly about driving in San Miguel. Regional differences exist.

A word about parking. Someone once asked me how my detective character always finds a parking place in San Miguel, especially when he's in a hurry on a case. That, I replied, is why it's called *fiction*.

The rules for driving in the countryside are not substantially different, although the hazards may be. Beyond city limits, Mexican traffic also operates by rational and coherent guidelines that are easily understood. These rules differ somewhat from those in the U.S. and Canada, much like cow sorting differs from dressage in horsemanship.

To illustrate this, a proper understanding of road signage in México is an excellent place to begin. Here we instantly encounter some cultural differences that require a closer look. The first point of difference is that of etiquette. Displaying directional signs at the side of the road is considered by many highway planners to insult the intelligence of the driver, even when he doesn't have the slightest clue where he's going. Second, the México Department of Transportation has as its motto: If You Don't Already Know How To Get There, You Have No Damn Business Trying to Go.

This is clear enough, and it encourages a healthy, independent–minded outlook on the part of the driver. No nanny state here, this is a country of hardy survivors who expect no help when navigating, and are therefore never disappointed.

Third, and possibly foremost, you will encounter the language problem. For example: you see a road sign that advises, *No Maneje Cansado. Evite Accidentes.* No problem, since you recall from high school Spanish thirty-one years ago that *cansado* means married. But wait, there is the idiom to consider, and you don't intend to be that easily tripped up. This obviously doesn't literally mean *Don't Drive While Married. Avoid Accidents.* You think for a moment: aha! Unmarried equals single, so it must translate as *Form Single Lane. Avoid Accidents!* This is not going to be as hard as you first thought.

Unfortunately, you have mistaken *cansado* for *casado*, and the first line of the sign means *Don't Drive While Tired.*

Perhaps driving in a single lane has something to do with animals you might encounter on the highway. You first catch sight of them as a herd of longhorn cattle at the edge of the blacktop two hundred meters further down the road. Prudently, you slow down a bit. But why is the cowherd sitting on a rock on your immediate right, grilling *nopales* (de-clawed cactus paddles), not even glancing in the direction of his herd? Fortunately they are showing no inclination to move on to explore the pavement, where there are only paper-thin sheets of road kill to eat anyway. Your reassuring recollection is that cattle here or anywhere are vegetarians.

You are slowly easing abreast of the herd when the possibility that something edible might be clinging to the practically dust-free surface of your three-month-old maroon BMW is too much for them to ignore. Is it only the alpine meadow smell of Bavaria still clinging within the wheel wells?

Soon you are surrounded with creatures that have very big wet lips and dangling tongues that could remove the seal coat from your finish with a single exploratory lick. These are tongues that could sweep the spines from a mature cactus without wincing.

Your hand leaps up to close your window, but it's already too late. As the lead cow presses its face to yours with an ingratiating expression, and rests its horns on the sunroof, it must have been the fertile overtones of its breath that made you lean on the horn as you did. As they scatter, your foot finds the gas pedal and spins you onto the opposite shoulder, narrowly missing a pair of overripe hindquarters about to add another element to this complex mix. As you streak up the highway, the tachometer seems to be measuring the rhythm of your heart.

Of course, on the other end of the spectrum, México is the home of the $80 car, as I mentioned elsewhere in this book. But having a modest purchase price is no excuse for having a wimpy sound system. It is not uncommon to find yourself at the wheel of your immaculate 5-series BMW behind a 30-year-old rust bucket that spent the most productive years of its life sliding sideways through the winters of Escanaba, Michigan. Vibrating even the pavement beneath your tires, the car's throbbing subwoofer feels as if it's also dissolving the nuclei right out of your brain cells.

Naturally, this was not the intent. You must never think of approaching the driver to complain, because his hearing was gone within hours of installing this system. Furthermore, the secondary purpose of it is to gradually work loose the accumulated rust from within his wheel wells. This accounts for the crunching sound under your crisp new Michelins as you follow him through traffic, even at a respectful distance.

Roadside chats among friends who pull over when

they meet behind the wheel are unknown in México. All conversations take place proudly in the middle of the street, especially when there is an opportunity to block both lanes. This is regarded as an occasion to demonstrate your social skills, your connectedness and standing in the community, and your personal clout rating. For many, it's a substitute for LinkedIn and Facebook. In this context, mere Tweets are unheard of. In México you cannot even say hello or goodbye in as few as 140 characters.

This country is the land of small-scale entrepreneurs running companies with no capital. Road services constitute a major example. Suppose you have come to a halt in the supermarket parking lot. Naturally you've angled your BMW across two spaces to protect it from dings. This brings a few dirty looks, but only from other gringos. The Mexicans correctly interpret this as an example of free style *parking*, a logical outgrowth of free style driving.

Immediately a young man rushes up with two buckets of fluid, offering to wash your car. A damp rag hangs over his shoulder. A word of caution is in order. This is his total water supply for the day. It is late afternoon and neither of the buckets looks especially inviting. The more opaque of the two contains not only a murky solution of road grime and liquefied diesel exhaust, but a volume of dissolved bird droppings equivalent to what you could extract from the bottom of a hundred Costa Rican parrot cages.

The bucket of "clean" water for rinsing is sufficiently polluted to deposit a milky glaze on your car that as it dries would bake like nacre in the sun. You are not remotely tempted, since you had never considered an opalescent finish as an upgrade for this car to begin with.

You graciously decline the boy's offer and slip him fifty pesos to guard the car while you're inside. It's worth it: he would've washed it for twenty.

Although it may be incomplete, since it does not cover all the subtle nuances of parking, which includes walking away from your car in the middle of the street when no parking spot is available, this still captures most of the fundamentals of driving in México. It is expressed with the kind of humor that is useful to maintain while driving here.

CHAPTER 7

HOUSES AND HOMES

At the end of the day we all have to come to earth somewhere. This is fundamental. Home is both our first stop and our last. Selling our homestead in Boise or Boston is painful, particularly after a long tenure where the kids were raised and launched. We need to know that our projected landfall in San Miguel is secure, free from challenge, and able to accommodate our accustomed lifestyle, approximately, even if it should take more than a few tweaks and adaptations to settle in. It will be the sturdy base from which we explore our new life. But how, exactly, can that be done with confidence when we have no experience of that new place, beyond the few visits that convinced us that it was a good idea to move there?

We will need to have some trust in the realtor we select, because that is where the search begins, and I will talk to a couple who have extensive experience here. But before I go there, I'd like to investigate the search process a bit more, just to include some aspects that northerners coming here to explore the market don't always think of. I have said elsewhere and I will say it again, that coming as we do from a different culture, whether Canada or the United States, it's hard to know what we're looking at here. On the ground, on a daily basis, things are different both in large scale and in detail. Isn't that one of the reasons we've decided to come? Yet, it is also one of our biggest risks.

Here is something to bear in mind: the style of home construction we have grown up with in the north comes from a much different tradition. With the first house I bought here, I paid $400 for an inspection (in 2007) and it failed to reveal a multitude of defects. I later accused the realtor of using his brother-in-law, and it may have been that he assumed some of those problems were expected, but I didn't think that. What it suggests to me is that we ought to use a house inspector who was raised with the same expectations that we were, because he will know our assumptions and understand where we're coming from.

Part of this issue is about usage and custom. Because this society is not crowded with people who can afford to hire every small-scale repair done by professionals, or even to buy the proper replacement parts, it has engendered an attitude that most people can (or, more likely, must) do everything themselves with improvised materials; whether it is plumbing, wiring, or masonry. So, you say your vintage Bentley has a problem with its fuel injection? My nephew will be there in the morning with farm tools and a reel of bailing wire. Just advance him the thirty pesos for the duct tape, if you will. He used up his last roll on the previous job fixing a shortwave radio.

This bit of hyperbole is less extreme than it first seems. In a housing boom, as was going on when my first house was built in 2004, many workers we might think of as unqualified found employment in construction, because, in addition to a shortage of experienced construction workers, as is well understood here, everyone knows how to do *anything*. Why bother to train people under those conditions?

Only, their skills just didn't work that well. Let me

think for a moment—should your doorsills and windowsills slope inward or outward when the rain hits them? Basic stuff, anyone would guess, so basic that you wouldn't think to check on it. And quite possibly, neither did the people who built your house.

The point of what follows is not to endorse anyone's businesses, but I chose to talk with several expats I knew who were focused on these issues and had been around long enough to address them from broad experience.

This is why an American from Walla Walla and Seattle, Washington, named Gordon Logan, has the niche business that he has. He and I spoke on a weekend day in April, Good Friday, in fact, when my car, parked three blocks up from his house, was about to be engulfed by a procession of reverent images and fervent people, moving along doing stations of the Cross at little shrines set up from house to house.

I started by asking Gordon whether he had been in the residential construction business in the States before he came down here.

"No," he said. "I spent thirty years in commercial real estate development and management, but I was always interested in homes and home improvement in Walla Walla. I knew how to read blueprints and I understood the mechanics of how things work."

"Then you must have been involved in building here in México, too, once you came."

"With this house where we're sitting we interviewed a dozen architects to find something that would work on a 22 by 164-foot lot. They all placed the entire house at the front of the street."

This *casa* sits on Calle 20 de Enero Norte, which makes up in genuineness what in lacks in obvious charm from the street view. It's a forthright working street, more mixed than it looks at first, but nonetheless full of expats and Mexicans making an active life for themselves. Building here, you would not want your day-to-day life fronting the busy sidewalk, and with the depth of this lot, there was surely no good reason to design it that way.

"And I didn't want a bowling alley at the back of the house. We decided that we'd design it ourselves and get someone to draw it up and build it. We divided it into four forty-foot pieces. We're very pleased with the way it went. During construction I was able to be here every day and make sure it was being built the way I wanted it to be."

If only we all could do that, but even if we could, how would we know that the materials and processes were the correct ones?

"After the house was done," Logan continued, "I realized that a lot of foreigners aren't able to be here all the time like I was, and that was a way I could add value to other people's experience. I decided to start Logan Construction Consulting. My first goal was to work with absentee owners who were having something built here. I've continued with that and expanded into other areas."

"When you moved to San Miguel, did you intend to continue working?"

"No." Logan shook his head, but with no sign of regret.

"What did you need for licenses or permits to be a house inspector?"

"First, I needed a Mexican work permit. It took a lot of effort to get that because there's nothing like real estate consulting or house inspections on their list of different occupations for issuing a work permit. Once I was able to describe the things I was going to do, they realized I wasn't going to be displacing any Mexican workers. Nobody was doing it then.

I brought a foreign perspective to the Mexican house. And because of my background I can relate more to the foreign homebuyer. After I started the consulting business, a number of realtors asked me if I would consider doing house inspections for their clients. I did quite a bit of research on the web on it. I contacted some friends, both realtors and architects in the U.S., to find out what requirements there were to be a home inspector. But there is no license required here."

"Do you have any employees?"

"No." His smile suggested he felt no loss from this.

"What has your experience been with the government, local or otherwise?"

"I have very few dealings with the government."

"Is your target customer a newbie?"

"No, but I do have lots of them. The majority of my time is spent with people buying existing homes in San Miguel. I try to invite the buyer to accompany me on the inspection. I explain how the house works. I talk about the electrical and plumbing, because as you know, houses work differently down here. I try to make them relax. Everyone has a little buyer's remorse no matter where they are. I try to make them feel comfortable with the house and answer any of their questions."

"Do you find you have to correct some people's expectations?"

"I try to modify them." Logan smiled broadly.

"A more diplomatic word. Who is your competition?"

"There's an architect here with an engineering background who does some inspections. He'll do a thirty-page report with lots of pictures, where my report is three or four pages. I think approximately the same conclusions are reached. I pride myself on being able to do an inspection in a couple of hours, more when necessary, but to also turn out a report in a couple hours after the inspection. That's really important to most buyers, because they put into their offer to purchase a contingency for the house inspection."

"By that time they're in motion."

"Yes."

"What's the largest difference between residential construction here and in the U.S.?"

"In the U.S., most of the construction is two-by-four walls with sheetrock. Down here the construction is cement beam and post with infill brick. The way the electrical work is installed, you have to chip out a channel to put in a conduit rather than fishing it through the walls. The plumbing is also different. We use cisterns down here many times with a *tinaco* (an open-topped water tank) on the roof with a pressure system, or just depend on city water, which is usually somewhat reliable."

"What kind of construction shortcuts are typically taken here?"

"In the electrical work there isn't a code that says you have to have grounding. Needs vary here, but they have become even greater in the eleven years I've lived in San Miguel. I go in and test every accessible electrical outlet to determine if they have grounding and proper polarity. I do that because we have large variances in our voltage here. Sometimes it can range between 90 and 140 volts. That can burn out a computer very easily, and then there are surges during lightning storms. You can put in a voltage regulator and a surge protector, but if your circuit is not grounded, that doesn't do any good."

"So when people see three holes in their outlet, and they know one is for the grounding pin, they still shouldn't assume that they're protected by grounding."

"That's right."

"Part of your task must be that of a translator,

explaining the construction standards of one culture to people coming down from another."

"Yes, and I try to do it in such a way as not to shock them, or to make them think that the house they're considering is a dump or something about to fall down. I explain the differences, and if it's a case of the electricity needing to be modified, for example, to explain how it should be."

"Are there issues of clear title here, and do you ever get into that?"

"I am a strong believer in title insurance, however it's not widely used here. You want to make sure that the title you're buying with this home can be legally conveyed to you. When you buy something here you have to go through a *notario*, and his office is obligated to search the title, but when I bought this property, I wanted to make sure that there was somebody else watching over the transaction, and that was the title insurance company."

Logan went on to explain that if the title insurance company declines to issue a policy, then you have essentially been given an opinion at no cost on how good the title is, and even if you don't know their reason for declining, you have still acquired some useful information in the process. If they won't assume the risk, neither should you.

"How would you compare your experience as a businessman here versus in the United States?"

"I have a lot more fun here. I really enjoy meeting the people and giving them an introduction to San Miguel."

Avoiding mistakes entirely is not possible, but the critical factor is to keep them small and capable of remedy. We come down to México to enjoy ourselves, to open doors to new events and activities in our lives, not to be occupied with trying to reverse the effect of our initial errors in judgment, especially when they could have been easily avoided. One thing I would strongly recommend is researching several different neighborhoods (*colonias*) you think you might like to live in. You can try to do this online only to a limited degree, but it is far better to do it in person on your visits before you move. That's the only way to begin to get the taste and feel of them.

Once you decide on the one you think you'd like to buy in, it is wise to rent there for at least six months first. Seriously, because driving or walking through even several times at different hours of the day will not really tell you what goes on there. You need to observe what it sounds like at three o'clock in the morning. You need to know the traffic patterns at different times of the day, and who your neighbors are.

Atención, our local bilingual weekly newspaper, lists the weekly crime statistics by neighborhood. What is the dog life like in the area you're thinking of? Will your delicate white Bichon Frisé on a leash be devoured on her first morning walk by a gaggle of feral street mongrels like some tidbit on a skewer? It is only possible to know these things when you spend some time there around the clock, and in more than one season. When you look at houses, consider also what I wrote about passive solar in the chapter titled **WEATHER**. Paying attention to this can have a critical impact on your mood, your comfort, and your heating bills while you live here.

Zoning as we have it in the States does not exist in San Miguel. I once looked at a beautiful house with great light and a large, but yet undeveloped garden space with terrific potential. It was also quite reasonably priced. Behind it was an ostensibly residential property being operated as an iron shop, and the clatter and pounding of hammers on metal started at eight o'clock in the morning and continued all day. It would have only been a good choice for a deaf couple that had no thought of resale.

Most people will prudently choose a house with a

garage or secure off street parking. Consistently leaving your car on the street overnight can invite problems. If the house you love lacks only this feature, you can often find a space to rent within a block or two nearby. This is not the handiest solution, but there are many cities in the U.S. where you would also need to do this.

If you buy a house with the bulk of its windows facing a vacant lot you will have NO protection against what might be built there. Your wall at any such lot should be blank on that side and your windows oriented (ideally) to the southwest in an unobstructed position. Otherwise a house could be built that blocks 90% of your daily sunshine and you would have no recourse. Your tropical flower garden may be reduced to an area fit only for growing moss and mushrooms. Your carefully aligned solar gain will be erased. If part of the charm is the view through the empty space across the street, you will have no way of guaranteeing it will continue without also buying that property yourself. When you look at your dream house, try to see its context in the future as well as how it looks now. The present is only a momentary snapshot, always subject to the whims of change. The best protection is that no vacant property exists around you.

Another option is to buy in a gated community that imposes design and use controls. There are quite a number of them, which testifies to their popularity. Especially if you are gone for part of the year, they will provide some basic protection for your property. House sitters exist, and some may be great, but they can also be a chancy lot. Some people will object that a gated community imposes a barrier between them and the real México, and in some ways it does. But the real México can easily be sentimentalized, and while it may be top heavy with mariachis in spiffy uniforms and flower-laden *señoritas* whose beauty can make your jaw drop, it can also mean exposure to nonstop fireworks all night during numerous fiestas, it can mean struggling with waves of graffiti passing through your neighborhood, or the casual tossing of bags of ripe garbage on your doorstep from the windows of passing cars.

Ask yourself for a moment why gated communities are equally popular with Mexican buyers as with expats. They often are a way of getting away, not from Mexicans specifically, but from certain kinds of behavior you don't want from your neighbors of any ethnicity. Do not assume either, that the expats you see here are always the classiest of people. As with many resort or vacation destinations, San Miguel draws all kinds, some of which you will wish had stayed at home. An old saw that is often repeated here goes like this: You are likely to be here either because you are wanted or you are not wanted. Think about it.

If the former owner or his tenant of a house you buy has left any unpaid utility bills, you will be asked to pay these yourself in order to get the service restarted in your own name. This can be a nasty surprise, and it would pay to go around before you close on the house and enquire at the phone company and other utilities. If you are building, make certain that the builder presents you with a receipt for his employee's social security benefits before you settle his final bill, because otherwise you can be held liable for them.

I will say once again, as I have said in other places, that the real secret of enjoying your experience of living in México is *managing your irritants*. In terms of preventing a bad outcome, this statement is worth a thousand times the price of this book. Study the neighborhood and the house you are thinking of taking on carefully. Talk to people who know the area. Master these issues and you will be the poster child for a blissful expatriate life.

Having offered these gentle admonitions, it's time to have a conversation with a realtor or two. I chose Claudine Langan, who's with Agave Sotheby's here, partly because she's successful in working with a diverse group of clients with varying needs, but also because she's Canadian and I wanted to be sure that perspective is represented. I have the sense, from the visitors I meet here, that the Canadian press has not spooked their readership with bad publicity to the same degree the American press has.

Claudine has a relaxed but professional manner, and her style is thoughtfully articulate. She and her husband live in a small, gated development about half a block down the street from me.

"In terms of the market," I began, "is this a good time to shop for a house in San Miguel?"

"Yes, it is. The market is heating up, and while it is still a buyer's market in most price points, we are seeing the tables starting to turn slightly in favor of the seller as inventory gets depleted, particularly in the $200,000 to $400,000 (U.S.) range. If this level of activity continues over the next year, the market will soon be favoring the seller."

I could already sense that we were coming out of a long trough here, where before not much was moving other than the very inexpensive homes and the high end ones. The middle has been static.

"To what degree is the market here linked to that in the U.S. or Canada?"

"The real estate market in San Miguel de Allende has historically, well, for the last several decades, anyway, been closely tied to those in Canada and the U.S., and that has not changed. This is why, in large part, the market is heating up here, because it is heating up in the U.S. and Canada too. That said, the strong Mexican economy and the growing middle class are also having a positive effect on San Miguel's real estate market. Though still closely tied to the U.S. and Canadian economies, the Mexican economy is also putting an upward pressure on real estate prices."

"What kind of services does the realtor provide for the buyer here?"

"That may depend on the realty company, but at Agave Sotheby's International Realty, we offer a full service experience, from start to finish. In addition to the obvious expectations of defining buyer needs and showing relevant properties, we closely manage the entire process in house purchasing, from the moment an offer is made to the moment the keys are handed to the buyer. We can do this because we have a staff lawyer who advises on taxes and legal procedures, two support staff who manage all the paperwork, and an accountant who advises on more complicated transactions. All a buyer working with us needs to do is define their needs and make their decision. We then turn that decision into homeownership."

"Is your typical house shopper Mexican, or an American or Canadian?"

"All of the above. And while the majority of our buyers are American, we have seen a definite increase in Canadian and Mexican buyers. Again, as these national economies stabilize and grow, we see an increase in all buyers. Also this year, we are seeing a few European and Asian buyers. Not many, but a few and we believe this segment of the business will continue to grow. This is new for San Miguel and we think it's due to increased global marketing of San Miguel de Allende and the heartland of México, and the growth of manufacturing happening in surrounding cities. Many of our Mexican and international buyers are coming from Querétaro, where automotive and aerospace manufacturing, for example, are on a steep growth trajectory. Other cities, like

Celaya, are attracting Asian executives with the automotive boom happening in that area, and these executives are drawn to the charms of San Miguel. Wealthy Mexicans from México City and Monterrey are also attracted to the simpler life here and are seeking second homes, a place the family can gather on weekends."

I had recently read that San Miguel has residents from forty different countries now.

"What are expats looking for in a house?"

"The vast majority of expats are looking for homes with colonial architectural features such as tall beamed ceilings, stone floors and window ledges, outdoor *salas*, covered porticos, central patios, views of the downtown. They want homes that ooze with charm, that feel old even if they aren't, and are unmistakably Mexican."

"Do you give people guidance as to one neighborhood over another?"

"First, I listen to what they say. For instance, some say they want to be in a neighborhood that has Mexicans and expats living side-by-side, while others say they would prefer a fully Mexican neighborhood, and still others prefer having mostly expats for neighbors. Once it is determined what kind of neighborhood they want, then I will guide them toward areas that I think they would be happy living in. Of course, budget also has a significant impact on which neighborhoods I can recommend and which I can't. But yes, part of my job is educating the buyer on the various areas, what they have to offer and which ones I think would suit their needs. Many of our buyers are not very familiar with San Miguel. A surprising number are on their first visit and only know the neighborhood they are staying in!"

"What do you say to that impulse buyer?"

"Well, that's an interesting question because we have

a lot of impulse buyers in San Miguel. The magic of this town often has an immediate seductive effect on people and before their two weeks of vacation are done, they have engaged a realtor and are spending their last few days looking at homes. I know a number of impulse buyers and, to my knowledge, none have any regrets. I was one of those buyers (bought a house the first time I came to San Miguel) and still, five years later, can't believe how lucky I am to live here, how beautiful my life is here. That said, I do encourage people to take their time to discover the various neighborhoods. They may only know the one they are staying in and may only want to look at homes in that area, but I try to expose them to other areas before they take the plunge."

"What are the pitfalls that buyers often miss?"

"I'm not sure this is a pitfall, but I think buyers get seduced by the charm of this town and may not take the time they need to make an educated decision. As I've said, the impulse buyer seems to do quite well in San Miguel but it's probably not the best way to buy a home. An expat buyer also has to remember that México is a foreign country and the real estate laws will differ from their own home country. So, it is absolutely critical that a buyer work with a well-informed real estate agent and agency. Showing people homes is a very small part of an agent's job and, frankly, not the most important. The most important role I have is to educate and guide my buyers through the legal and financial processes and lead them to a smooth and successful closing. Once a buyer has chosen his or her dream home, my real work starts!"

"How easy is it to buy a house in San Miguel?"

"Buying in San Miguel is surprisingly easy. In fact, in many ways it is easier than the experience an expat may have had in their home country. The main reason for this is that the vast majority of real estate transactions are done in cash here, eliminating the onerous demands of banks and mort-gages. The paperwork is comparatively minimal as well and the entire process, from the moment an offer is made to the moment the keys are handed over, can be done in as little as two weeks. Our typical closing period—from offer to close—is around four to five weeks."

"In addition to the price of the house, what other costs are involved?"

"In San Miguel, the seller is responsible for pay-ing all realty fees and the buyer is responsible for paying the legal fees. The legal fees range between 1.5% and 1.7% of the sales price."

Knowing what I know now, it still always alarms me to think about those impulse buyers and what they might be letting themselves in for. Not that I don't applaud the ability to take chances, but being more informed can save the buyer a world of headaches.

Several weeks after this conversation I met with Nancy Howze of C/D/R San Miguel Real Estate Agency. It was a cloudy morning in June and the sky threatened to open at any moment. People who live here always try to applaud that because we need the rain, but it's often too hard not to wonder where the sun went, we're so spoiled by sunny skies.

Nancy is a tall blonde with a deep Alabama twang that some might think sounds like Texas. I made some coffee and we chatted for a while about the reader this book was aimed at. I try to give the people I talk to a sense of who might be listening to their conversation.

"A lot of local people will buy this book to see who's in it that they know. There are also chapters on sub-jects where they may not feel they're fully up to speed, like HEALTH CARE, for example, which I know is going to be one that many people turn to first. But mainly this book is aimed at Americans or Canadians who might be daydreaming about moving to México and wondering where to land, or some who are two years away from retirement and further along in that process, who might be taking a hard look at San Miguel. There also may be some who have already moved to México, and after three hot summers are wondering if they should have settled on the beach to begin with, and whether a higher altitude, where it cools off at night, might have been a better choice."

"Well, I hope that whatever comments I make will have some value to someone who is considering living here. I just sold a house within the last couple of months to a Canadian couple that had earlier purchased a place at the beach, in Baja California on the Sea of Cortez. They're moving here now because their experience was that there was no culture there. You get up in the morning, you walk on the beach, you come home and you play on the Internet, you have lunch, you have a drink, you have dinner and you go to bed. You get up in the morning, you walk on the beach, and so on. San Miguel has so much to offer that, for me, it's a wonderful place to live. I can go rent a house at the beach if I want to, if I need a little water fix after living in the high mountain desert for a while. I think San Miguel attracts a lot of different people, but it also attracts people that have an adventurous spirit."

"I think that most of us who have moved here," Nancy continued, "probably have more things in common than we might realize, because we're all people that have *left*. We've left our families and hometowns where we worked and grew up, where we have a core group of friends, to have another adventure. There are people that might be moving here so that they can have a better life (on less money than in the U.S.), but I also think that people move here because they're ready for another chapter in their lives."

"You mean that because our life expectancy is stretching out, they have a longer time after their working life ends, and they're looking for meaningful ways to use it."

"Exactly. We now have a longer retirement time that we didn't always have before. There are lawyers that come down here and become painters. They use a totally different side of their brain than what they used in their business career. San Miguel really allows you to be whoever you want to be here. One of the things that I found is that this is a welcoming, inclusive community. It's easy to find your place here."

"Not every place is as welcoming," I said. "It's hard enough to pick up your life and transplant it, so it's good to know the soil here is accommodating."

"Well, for example, take Charleston, South Carolina. If you decide to move there at age sixty-five, it is a very closed city, socially. You're not going to be a Charlestonian unless your family has been there for at least five generations. San Miguel offers something 180° away from that. You bump into somebody in a restaurant having lunch or dinner at the next table and you start up a conversation, and before you know it you're going over to their house for a drink or having a meal there some time in the next week. It's *inclusive*."

"Isn't part of that simply the fact that we are all expats? When you come here and get off the bus or the plane, you are instantly part of that context and the expat community. You might have to work just a bit to dig it out, but it is there waiting for you."

"I think you're absolutely right, and because we've all left, we more easily become family to each other. We have left our past, even our long-term friends and family and associations with others behind, so to me, it's lovely because of that context."

"Let's talk about your background and how you came

into the realty business."

Nancy stirred her coffee thoughtfully. "Interestingly enough, real estate is the only thing I've ever done twice. I was a realtor in the United States. For many years, I did other things too, and I'm actually a retired school teacher, at the high school level." She went on to describe a wide variety of other careers she'd had, all in Alabama. If they didn't always seem connected to each other, in the aggregate, they amounted to a range of skills that had to be helpful in the realty business, since they would've brought her into contact with a wide variety of business people. There are few careers more people-oriented than real estate, since you are facing clients daily whose main goal is to come to earth.

"Then I got into real estate in the late 1980s and worked in that field for quite a while before I moved here in 1998 to retire and not do anything. I didn't do anything for about six years, and then got back into real estate in San Miguel in 2004. I have found that doing it here is totally different than in the United States. Not that my skills in that market haven't served me well here, but the process is so different, the way it's done. When I first arrived here, I thought, what is going on? It was just crazy. But it has become, over the sixteen years that I've lived here, more like the U.S. than it was. The realtors are now cooperating with each other, while they really weren't back then. If you were a buyer you almost had to go to every real estate company. They didn't share their listings with each other, so you didn't know what was on the market."

"And therefore there was no overview. That didn't serve the buyer very well, did it? It must have made for a lot of leg work and redundancy."

"It didn't serve the buyer *or* the seller. When I first moved here I thought, you know, being a trained realtor, you work for the seller, since that's where your fiduciary responsibility is, because the seller is the one paying the commission. That's the one who has hired you to sell his house. When I came here I just decided that all the agents were only working for themselves. But it has changed dramatically over the last ten years since I got back into it. Realtors are now cooperating with each other, they understand the value of doing that, and just from a business perspective, I can sell a lot more real estate when I cooperate with other agents in town. As opposed to just having my own listings and concentrating on only selling those. So it's really getting to be a lot more like the United States."

"What trends have you seen in house values over the ten years since you came back into the business. Has it been cyclical?"

"It has certainly been up and down. It had been going up and up, and probably the peak was 2007 to the start of 2008, and then the crash came in the fall of 2008 and everything changed. If you bought a house at the top, what happened was that because almost every transaction is cash here, nobody has a mortgage. When people in the U.S. lost a lot of money on their houses, they started looking around and asking how they could replace that loss. Maybe they owned a house here and considered it a static asset, so suddenly the San Miguel inventory went up dramatically."

"Because people were gathering the wagons, pulling back. One answer was to be cashing out here," I offered.

"Yes, people were selling their homes here and trying to reinvest that money. All of a sudden the inventory just blew up and it instantly became a buyer's market. Then those prices came down. They are slowly going back up now. It's not a rocket, but it is a slow progress. This year has been the best year since 2009. We're having a lot of sales. Prices have come back up and are stabilizing. Inventory is getting sold, so it's coming off the market. It has been a gentle climb, but there was a big fall in 2008-9."

"Let's look at who your typical buyer is now and how do you find them? Or rather, how do they find you?"

"It happens both ways. As you probably know, many people, probably eighty to ninety percent of the buyers, are looking online. But one of the things that often happens to people is that they come to San Miguel for a vacation, or for a wedding. It's a huge wedding destination too. And then they fall in love. It's not unusual for somebody to come for a week with no intention of buying and suddenly they're signing a contract. That is not a rare story."

"But is that a *good* story?" As usual, this was a narrative that was scaring the hell out of me, knowing what I know, what I've written about in the earlier part of this chapter. I thought buying on impulse here was about as safe as buying a camel in Libya online, one you have never met or ridden, whose feed and veterinary bills you have never seen, just because the beast looked charming and even romantic, and took good photos to send back home. Then there was the cost of that peculiar saddle, and that odd bridle made by Bedouins. The annual worming, and so on. It was nothing you ever thought of.

"You know, I'm not sure I can answer that question. You're asking it from the point of view, of whether that is a good way to do things."

"Yes, I am, because part of what this book is about is *preparedness*, the old Boy Scout motto. If you're coming down here, then be prepared. Do your homework. You wouldn't try to service your own car without the manual, so why would you blindly try to service your own life without doing some research when it came to taking a turn like this?"

"Well, here's one thing I have observed. There are

leapers and there are creepers. I am a bit of a leaper myself. I knew I wanted to live outside of the U.S. I wanted a new adventure. I was at a point in my life where I had been a single parent. Then my kids were gone and it was *my* turn to go. I came down here once for a week, went back home and sold my house, and then moved here. I thought, 'What's the worst that can happen?' But I did not buy anything then, I rented first, although I was here six weeks and I bought a piece of property and started building a house. I am a bit of that person who runs to the end of the diving board and jumps off and checks if there's any water in the pool on the way down. I know that is not everyone's personality. Some people are much more detailed in wanting to do all their homework. If you took a poll of all those who came down and made an immediate decision, whether they are still happy with it after five years, I don't know. Maybe some are not. Maybe they didn't buy in the neighborhood they now would like to be in."

We were silent for a moment. Part of this issue was how to proceed with your life at a given point. I have never been a guru, nor wanted to be. There are other books that offer that. I went back to practical.

"Does the realtor have a role in educating the buyer?"

"Absolutely. The realtor has a role to play in educating them, but I am often asked by buyers, 'What do you think?'"

"They're asking you to tip them one way or another."

"That's right, but at the end of the day, it's not my money, and not everybody thinks the way I do. So just as the realtor has a responsibility to educate, the buyer has a responsibility to ask intelligent questions. I don't like to be judgmental because we're not all looking for the same experience here. Some want to be in a gated community. Others what to be in neighborhoods where there are more Americans around them. Others want to be in a mixed neighborhood with people who have grown up and lived in San Miguel forever. When I talk to a buyer I like to talk first about the process."

"But there must be some very common mistakes buyers make."

"In terms of what are the most common mistakes buyers make here, one is that sometimes people leave their brain at the border. My advice is, bring it with you."

"Because there's no duty on it." We had to pause for a moment while she imagined this. We had all crossed at Laredo at some point.

"I have heard of and known of people who came down here and wrote a down payment check directly to the realtor. You wouldn't ever do that. To me that's a huge example. Don't do anything you wouldn't do at home. It's also important to think about, whatever you get into, what is your exit plan? It doesn't matter—Oh, I love this house, I'm going to live here forever—but you're not. You may live there until you die, but somebody else is going to have to sell it. So you always need to know whether you're doing the right things to take care of yourself on the back end. None of us knows what's around the corner. We may think we're going to stay down here for the rest of our lives. But something may happen and we may need to sell our house for whatever reason."

I know that some people do plan to die here, and others die here who haven't planned it that way. It's partly about how they see themselves. Are they immigrants with their feet planted here, or are they vacationers or part timers, where the final bell will always ring for them over the border to the north? For myself, I'd prefer to end it here, where it all came alive for me after a lifetime of long winters too close to Canada. The reader of this book should think about that question too, although it may be too early to answer it in many cases.

"I love my life here," Nancy went on. "It's so much richer than it would be if I were still in the U.S. I do know that people come here and live on fixed incomes and don't intend to work and make money. But goodness, I don't go to the grocery store. I have a cook. Because we can have staff, it frees up my time to do what I want to do."

"So, I have written earlier in this chapter about the reasons for choosing a gated community, as you did at Candelaria. Do you have a sense of what the proportion is of Canadian and American residents to Mexican residents there?"

"In Candelaria, it's fascinating. There are no Canadians. But we have many more Mexicans than Americans. This year (writing this at the end of June) I have sold four properties there, and three of them went to Mexicans."

This is where I wanted to finish this conversation, because I had looked at gated communities earlier. We were quiet for a while as Nancy finished her coffee. She looked out over my patio, where we had ripped out the thirty-foot bamboo that was our way of thumbing our noses at Minnesota weather, and replaced it with native plants. It was an affirmation of the place where we had settled, rather than a rejection of what we had left.

"I sense there's something more you want to add," I said.

"Yes, there is. Buyers coming down here to look at property should be selective about who they pick as their agent. If they're happy with one, they should stick with that one. It gets confusing for everybody if they jump around. Now that the entire real estate community is cooperating, you're not limited in your ability to see everything that's out there in your price range. You should work with someone whose personality works with yours, one you feel comfortable with, where you're getting good and honest answers. It's not always going to be the biggest company or the smallest. We have a lot of good realtors in this community."

Once again, Access San Miguel will provide a list of those realtors.

CHAPTER 8

FULFILLMENT HAS A MEXICAN ADDRESS

In the previous chapter, Nancy Howze brought up the idea of people moving down to San Miguel and taking a sharp turn off their own beaten path, for example, the lawyer who becomes a painter when he arrives and discovers how to use a different side of his brain. I looked briefly at the same process in the last paragraph of the first chapter, WHY SAN MIGUEL? Moving here acts like a door opening, but first there is often a period of reassessment, either before or after arrival.

In this process, some people will take stock of their lives after a long career in business. Perhaps it was in law, as above, or in health care. Beyond business success in itself, what worked? What didn't? What was missing? The focused effort of achieving success in one field often comes at the cost of neglecting something else, or even many other things. I'm always fascinated with articles by end-of-life caregivers who talk about the regrets people express on their deathbeds. A common one is that they worked too hard and didn't spend enough time with their families, or in activities that would have better enriched their lives.

Others arrive here with a bucket list. If it's not in their wallet, it might still be in the back of their mind. Go to

Machu Picchu, check. Go on safari, check. Set a world record for something…but what? They'll have to figure that one out.

It's about gaps, and it's about dreams. If we haven't fulfilled all our dreams, at least we remember them while there's still time to address them. But life can have a way of inserting roadblocks into the dream landscape. Marriage as a reality may match the dream image, but often does not. The kids might not be what we hoped. Maybe the grandkids will be more rewarding. At least you can walk away from them at the end of the day. Maybe you were downsized before you were ready to retire. The company you gave so much to now no longer needs you. They replaced you with someone less than half your age making half your salary. Or maybe you just couldn't stand the rat race anymore. What comes next?

Fulfillment can be elusive. We've all made our choices, and we've heard that life offers no second chances. But like a lot of things, that's only true if you believe it. I want to take a look at some choices our family has made, and how being in San Miguel is an important part of that, and why.

As a teenager my wife, Kristine, loved horses. She rode whenever she could. But then came college, with its heavy financial and time demands, then marriage, a medical technology career, and then kids. Soon she realized she'd cantered off on a different trail, almost without deciding to, and that the nearly unnoticed fork in the road she had taken was by that time a long way behind her.

Kristine took an early retirement when we left Minnesota. As I have mentioned, we are wrapping up our seventh year living in México. She began riding again three years ago by saying, "I think I'm going to take five lessons, just to see if it's still fun."

I won't go through the process of how those five lessons blossomed into the ownership of a Lusitano mare named Martina, a Schleese dressage saddle, numerous pieces of tack and riding outfits. We have learned that anything on which the word *horse* appears costs three times as much as the same thing unlabeled. That was a hard lesson, but the easy lesson is that an engaging, and even compelling pastime of forty years ago is still available as an absorbing part-time career later in life. Sometimes the things you walked away from, even for sufficient reason, may still be there awaiting your return. An important question to ask is whether those things are open-ended. Is the potential for further growth larger than the time we have to pursue it? Like the arts, horsemanship offers that growth potential. After all, we did not come down here to bump the edges, to trace the limits of our lives. Quite the opposite.

Kristine has pulled on her breeches, half-chaps and tiny little blunt spurs again, tightened the strap of her helmet, and she's riding four days a week at the Rancho San Miguelito near the pilgrimage village of Atotonilco. Martina had been a popular brood mare for several years, and with all the duties of motherhood, had lost some of the polish of her early training, but Kristine was able to ride her three times a week for nearly a year before she bought her. Those two already knew each other well when she came up for sale, and Martina had recovered most of her skills in the process. She is now a natural athlete with a weakness for carrots. If you ask Kristine, she will say that you *can* go back, just as she picked up the dropped reins, put her feet back into the stirrups, and rode off, not into the sunset, but into a fresh morning in the Mexican countryside.

She's also gotten involved in jewelry making, constructing unique pieces of her own design, and she's learned to do interior book design for San Miguel Allende Books, my own publishing company. If you are reading a print copy of this book, an example of her work is in your hands.

In some ways, my story offers a few interesting parallels, at least in terms of long interruptions. I came out of college with a degree in creative writing and was hired as a salaried writer in mental health for the State of Minnesota Welfare Department, even while I worked on two novels. But mental health drove me crazy and the novels didn't work out. That was my roadblock, my fork in the road, and I walked away from writing by choice, thinking I couldn't do that much work and spend a year's time writing a book only to have the outcome be unsatisfying. I also didn't care to stay with a writing job I disliked, one where every journal article I wrote featured my name in last position behind three people who outranked me, but hadn't done any of the writing. I also walked away from my job at the State of Minnesota.

What I found however, was that writing had not walked away from me, and over the years I heard it tapping away now and then at an abandoned keyboard somewhere inside my head. Try again, a small voice kept saying, try again. And I did, six or seven times, each one several years apart, but I failed to reengage every time, and I found myself unable to complete anything more demanding than a grocery list for thirty-seven years.

Still, I did a number of other interesting things. I started a company that built custom-made furniture on my own designs. I constructed paneled rooms and restaurant interiors. In 1982, I built the landmark Times Bar at the corner of 11th and Nicollet in Minneapolis. It was a popular watering hole for years until the building was leveled to put up a high rise. I took up painting and even did some successful portraits, a task I often thought would be the most daunting of all. But fulfillment, at least in the direction of writing, which I had never entirely forgotten, remained a pipe dream of the most elusive kind.

LIVING IN SAN MIGUEL

I was on a painting trip in New Mexico early in July of 2005. Driving down the long serpentine slopes of the Carson National Forest on the way into Taos, a scene from a mystery came to me. That same day, at the hotel where I was staying, I wrote that scene, and found that the visceral reaction I'd had in the past every time I tried to write something did not reappear. The barrier was gone, and the door stayed open.

When the writer's block ended so unexpectedly that day, I began the first of my San Miguel mysteries, titled *Twenty Centavos*. There are twelve of them now. Was it México that made this happen for both of us? No. We did it ourselves because we decided to do it. But México is a *simpatico* place where such things can more easily happen, and San Miguel is a hospitable backdrop against which to tinker with the direction of your life. A little more this way, a little less that way, might be the roadmap to fulfillment. You won't know until you try. It's out there waiting. The large expatriate community here makes for an ample support group to ensure a soft landing on arrival. You can get up and start dancing.

Wondering about that process, in the first year after I moved here, I had conversations with thirty-two people who had made this kind of change. They had upended their lives in the United States and Canada and settled here full time in San Miguel. I told them that, even though I'd done it myself, I wasn't sure I fully understood why other people would do this. Were their reasons the same as mine? The result was unexpected. I discovered as many different reasons to move here as there were people I talked with. There was no common expat 'type.' Each story was different, and some were startling. The people who did this chose themselves. You could not take 500 people at random from the streets of Wichita or anyplace else and get the same outcome. You have to both want and need to do it.

"What about security?" I asked in these conversations. Already by this time the American media was beating the drum constantly about México being a dangerous place. From our travels all around the country by bus and car, Kristine and I both knew that there was no special risk to living here. We did then and still do what Americans do at home—we understand where the trouble spots are, and we avoid them. That's all that is required to lead a perfectly safe and normal life. The local expatriates I spoke with confirmed this. Still, I regularly hear from others who've been spooked by the U.S. media and the State Department, and are afraid to even visit. I tell them that the odds are they are safer here than they are at home in the U.S.

The book that came from these conversations was *San Miguel de Allende: A Place in the Heart.* It's my effort, not at explaining the expatriate experience here, but at illustrating it, showing how it operates day by day.

Something I learned from those conversations, and from my own experience since, is that the door is open here, even if in the past you were the one who kept it closed yourself, as I did. Your arrival in San Miguel is permission to change and grow. It's a ticket.

Fulfillment can mean many things. One thing I know for certain about it is that it doesn't chase you. I think that change, any change, is a stimulus that helps make it possible, and a change like moving to México may open some doors on aspects of ourselves we may have thought were lost. For others, it may give them unexpected access to a totally new way of life in the future. Being in a different country causes some of our self-imposed limitations to fall away. We will find that people don't have the same expectations of us, and that is a new freedom in itself—the freedom to be different from what we once were. I've always believed in the possibility that we can reinvent ourselves. México is a great place to do it.

I know that Kristine agrees with me that we have come to earth here. We could never go back. It has a seductive charm in the people, the arts, and the culture that's become irreplaceable to us. México is our home.

CHAPTER 9

MY NEIGHBORHOOD

Suppose, that after considerable due diligence, you have selected your San Miguel neighborhood, the one where you think you'd like to buy a home once you've gotten to know it, and have rented a house there for six months. Let us further say that you have not chosen a gated community, but instead, a mixed one. You have some ideas about how you'd like to connect with your neighbors and you would prefer that they not be just like the ones you left behind in Salem, Oregon, although, naturally, you will feel more comfortable with some expats in that mix.

This more or less describes our attitude when my wife and I moved to San Miguel. We wanted to be part of a community that offered an experience different from home, one where we could feel more connected than we did in Edina, Minnesota. At that time, lacking a book like this one, we did not understand the very good reasons for renting first, so we bought our first house immediately.

Somewhat later, we now live in the neighborhood called Colonia Caracol (snail). Our house stands about fifty meters beyond a five-street intersection, of which three streets are major: Cinco de Mayo, Prolongacíon Aldama, and Camino al Caracol, which winds up the hill and empties onto the *libramiento*, the beltline highway that wraps around most of this town. The remaining two streets wander off into other small *colonias.*

The entire area is built on a fairly steep slope, so it's easy to leave, and the walk to the *jardín* is brisk and refreshing. Coming back in mid afternoon following a big pasta lunch with two glasses of wine is better accomplished in a taxi.

Naturally, owning a house on a slope like this provides some long views. Ours reach over and past the reservoir, the *presa*, into the mountains nearer Guanajuato, the state capital. We can't see the Parroquia, the church that fronts the main plaza, downtown. A scattering of power lines interferes slightly with this view, but the buriers of utility cable are approaching, and have reached the intersection directly below us. Over the southern end of the city, two or three hot air balloons often pass in the morning on the way to wherever nature is going to take them that day.

The Caracol neighborhood is about 85% Mexican, ranging from crushingly poor to quite wealthy. The expats fall somewhere between. At the crest of the hill stands the Caracol condominiums, a building that grows to five stories tall as it descends the slope. It was controversial during construction because nothing else in the city was built quite on that same scale. The façade was given neocolonial detailing to appease the protesters, although the buyers of the condos, being mostly from Querétaro and México City, would have been perfectly happy with a more contemporary look. All the wealthier Mexicans of the neighborhood are concentrated in this building, but are only in residence chiefly on the weekends and holidays. To some degree, for some people, San Miguel is a getaway town, which suggests it offers some features that the larger cities of México do not.

The colonial style trim that was applied to the Caracol condominium façade, and is offered on most new construction here, consists of *cantera* stone door and window surrounds, with a molded cornice at the top floor. Its charm is admired more by expats than the locals, who do not generally feel that the 1750 look is sufficiently cutting edge, even though it works well on buildings that are actually of that era. To most expats, however, it looks like Europe on the cheap, with a texture and feel clearly different from the strip malls, 1950s suburbs, and skyscrapers they left at home. As someone who always thought he would end his days in France or Italy, and whose dream of a Mediterranean retirement was wiped away by a dollar better suited to wallpaper than European prices, the look of this town suits me fine.

In a larger sense, the colonial style is derived from ancient Roman and even Greek models, and as a longstanding approach toward living in one's house with a relationship to nature, it is, in my view, difficult to beat. It has a certain private grace to it, a sense of form in its arches and domes, its high ceilings, its fountains and courtyard gardens, and in the character of its shadows, that we abandon only at our own loss. The modern version of the severe 1930s Bauhaus style, all angles and slabs, a trimless machine age look, has no place in my view of this country, yet it is the basis of much popular current Mexican residential architecture.

Within less than a kilometer from my front door are four schools, ranging from kindergarten through high school. The elementary school and the middle school run in double shifts. This explains a somewhat larger than normal police presence during school hours, a phenomenon no one appears to object to. While the school walls are often targets of graffiti, it has never reached this far up the hill. What does get this far, borne on the wind, is band practice—both of their featured tunes—and the occasional stem winder of a speech to the assembled students. At six weeks, summer vacation is too short, not only for the students, but for us as well.

This is all part of the kind of engagement that comes from having my office on the second floor terrace of my house. Since this working space is open on three sides, the life of the principal intersection of this community has become my life too. Five steps away from my desk—a round, weathered *equipale* table with pigskin top and slatted sides—I can lean over the parapet and watch the variegated drama of San Miguel street life below. It runs in shifts bounded by the catch and release of the two daily school sessions, the morning water and gas deliveries, and the homemade ice cream wagon in the afternoon. It is punctuated by the comings and goings of the neatly dressed office crew of the Caja Popular across the street. This is the regional administrative office, so it attracts no customers, and therefore little traffic.

More seasonal are the sound trucks touting the touring circus, and in election years the sound trucks touting the political candidates. Even the scrap dealers are wired for sound, buying your copper, your steel, your old stove, or your aluminum cans. It reminds me of growing up in North Minneapolis in the 1950s, where the scrap dealer, without amplification, made his rounds through the alleys in the last horse-drawn wagon I ever saw in that or any other modern town in the States. But then that is another feature of this country—we do not find ourselves uniformly in the twenty-first century here. Time can be warped in surprising ways.

Looking around this neighborhood, it does not appear to be very old. The house I now live in was built ten years ago and there are many others nearby of the same vintage. Yet, there are also signs of earlier inhabitants, earlier uses. This is a country where Western European civilization is an overlay, a graft, and deeper traditions easily endure beneath the skin.

To the north of my property is an unbuilt lot, and, in expectation of another house going up some day, my house is blank unpainted stucco on the side that faces it. My light comes from the other side, entering over my courtyard from the southwest, with abundant passive solar energy. The owner of this vacant lot stores timbers and other construction materials there. This is not unusual. It's a workaround until a buyer or a better use appears. Beyond that yard is the unpretentious house of a man who is an expert upholsterer, and at the same time, a neighborhood counselor. This corner marks the edge of the barrio, a wedge of haphazard improvised buildings that climb the steep slopes in the shape of a fan, with the widest part at the top. This is the home of the poorest people in the neighborhood. Many houses are makeshift constructions with dirt floors and corrugated sheet metal walls. I have heard that some of these residents are squatters, but there's no good way to make certain, no polite way to ask. I prefer to respect the privacy of their tenuous hold on home ownership. It is not unusual to see this wide variety of structures within a small neighborhood. Sticking to your own kind is not a high priority.

At the other side of the barrio entrance stands a tall red house of about the same vintage as mine. It belongs to a couple from Oregon. They are in a unique situation because their double garage on the main floor is built on sacred ground, which is what made me think of those earlier inhabitants. Our neighbors have an agreement with the indigenous people, whether the Otomí or the Chichimeca, I don't know, to give them access to it for special occasions, such as the ceremony I once found myself looking at as I stood in the middle of the street, and in the middle of the night. An arroyo, a deep drainage ditch runs under this intersection. Except for storm runoff, it's usually dry. Saying good morning all around, I joined the other people sitting on the parapet edging it and I watched the proceedings. In the darkness, the glowing aura from the open steel garage doors suggested a sacred grotto within.

The garage was decorated inside with a coarse fabric draping the walls like bunting. In the center of the back wall, placed high enough to be seen by all the crowd, was a portrait of a man of middle age, with ample hair down to his collar and long sideburns. He wore a suit jacket but no tie, and an uncomfortable look, as if he had only dressed for the photo and would quickly be changing afterward.

A neighbor told me that this was the *Velación* of the Virgin of San Juan. *Velación* usually refers to a wake, but no body was present. She said it was a family tradition, and the portrait on the wall was a family member revered by his community, who'd been dead for many years. At the back of the garage stood dozens of vases of calla lilies. I couldn't see much more of what was going on, and I didn't feel like elbowing my way in. Taking any photos was out of the question. And who was the Virgin of San Juan? The mother of Christ has many manifestations here, but this was one I hadn't heard of. Nor did it appear to be terribly clear to the neighbors around me in the intersection. But it was a good show and it was free, even if it was staged at three A.M. Beyond that, they really didn't know much about it. People work hard here, and entertainment is valued, even when it's not always clear what it means.

This was not the first time I'd seen otherworldly events at this double garage. One evening the doors opened and a hoard of indigenous dancers in full regalia came prancing and twirling out, feathers flying, drums pounding. There was no sign of the gray Toyota SUV that was normally kept there.

Offering a place to park cars and occasionally hold religious rituals is not all that garages can do. Often they host small hole-in-the-wall stores (*tiendas*) that feature fruits and vegetables, snacks and soft drinks. A further use, and double garages are the preferred venue for this, is for wakes.

Even though the law no longer mandates it, burial or crema-
tion is still generally carried out within twenty-four hours of
death. Embalming is not often done among poorer families.
All through the night you can hear the singing and chanting
as the deceased lies in state among flowers, candles, garden
equipment, used tires, and garbage cans. Rows of borrowed
folding chairs are provided. It has a bittersweet and realistic
effect; a farewell framed so intimately among the implements
of life.

In the morning, the coffin is closed and lifted onto the
shoulders of friends and family and carried down Cinco de
Mayo to the main cemetery, the Pánteon, which is just a block
on the other side of Ancha de San Antonio. One morning,
standing on my terrace, I heard a group of mariachis start up,
and coming down the slope I saw a large crowd of mourners
carrying *three* coffins. Astounding! It must have been a tragic
traffic accident that took out three family members at once.

Other than a gathering place for fiestas, funerals, and
other recurring ceremonies, our little intersection is during
the day a forum for business. At breakfast and lunch an older
woman sets up a grill and sits on the parapet of the arroyo
in her apron while she makes *gorditas* and other specialties
for meals on the fly. We have paid to send two of her three
children to high school. One is about to start college in
Saturday morning sessions. They have the ambition to move
up and out of the grip of poverty.

We know many of the kids and the dogs here by name.
In the afternoon, a table goes up under an umbrella three
meters away offering prepared treats, sticks of jicama dipped
in powdered chili, fruit drinks in plastic bags with straws,
gelatin in plastic cups, cubed pineapple and other fruits. Every
day is a working day and every place is potentially a place
of business.

The upholsterer I mentioned above occupies a position in this small community that has, I believe, no direct equivalent in the U.S. or Canada. He is in a commanding location to watch the comings and goings of the barrio, and he knows the players at all levels. When we leave on vacation we let him know before we go. "*Un ojo*," he responds solemnly, touching his eyelid with a sly look and pointing at our house. He will be watching. Early this year when my wife was in the U.S. for her mother's 85th birthday, he came over and enquired whether everything was OK. He had not seen her, he said, for four or five days. *Un ojo*, I thought as I explained where she was and thanked him for his concern. *One eye is watching.* That is not surveillance, it's community.

At other times I will see him seated on the stone parapet, a kind of crude community bleacher. He will be head to head with a roughly dressed man from the country, or a town laborer, listening carefully and offering advice. His expression says that he takes all comers seriously, that he gives them the best counsel he can summon, which I suspect is very good indeed. It must be grounded in his faith, as well as his experience, because on his doorframe is a plaque with a terse warning: *Somos Catolicos!* In other words, no missionaries are welcome in this house, we are Catholics here. Even so, common sense and clear thinking have to be the ballast that anchors his consular role in our *colonia*.

And how well do we two expats from the distant north country fit in with this complex brew? Or do we at all? The answer is yes and no. Our goal has always been to be good neighbors, if not close friends, because the cultural, social, and financial divides between us can amount to a forbidding set of barriers. Many of our neighbors are stiffly formal with us, because they feel that as foreigners, we must be rich. To some degree, we will never fit in, and that's all right. We did not come down here to become Mexicans, but to live in México among Mexicans. Our neighbors are rarely big travelers, and to most of them we might seem a bit exotic, even though they have seen their share of expats before. How many servants do we have, they wonder. They are shocked to discover that we have none, other than the gardener that comes for three hours every two months. Often, we have let them observe us more closely, just as we have sought to demonstrate that we respect their culture and values, even when they know we are not always believers in the same way that they are.

Somehow, based on mutual respect and good will, this approach has always worked out.

CHAPTER 10

FIESTAS

As I write this on my second floor terrace, where I've written about fifteen other books, the cobblestone street below me has been in preparation by neighborhood volunteers all day. A grid of posts has been anchored by digging out some of these stones, a civic desecration that could never occur on the tarmac of a U.S. town. Arches have been erected to connect them, and a street surface painting of a star and crown motif executed in brilliantly dyed sawdust awaits the procession of the Holy Cross from up on the hill. Here the march to Calvary goes down, not up. Torrents of flowers crown every structure. I contributed to the floral fund for today's ceremony, as I have for years. We will be down on the street when it comes together. These are some of the ways we fit in San Miguel, by making it clear that we support local culture in this very mixed neighborhood.

The Aztec dancers have already arrived in exotic dress, both men and women. I can't tell whether they have just left their ancient homes at the restored pyramid out at la Cañada de la Virgen (nothing whatever to do with Ottawa), just outside of town, or whether this exotic crowd is partly composed of my lawyer and my car mechanic, with the woman who handles my car insurance, and her younger sister who checks out my groceries at the Mega Market. It doesn't seem to matter now. Their headdresses especially are vivid with color and long feathers, some dyed, some not, often resembling the pheasant tails that I recall from Minnesota cornfields in the fall. Their costumes are often riveting, just as the drums are deafening as they work up the crowd, and I can barely hear to write this. At the end of the block across the street a welded grid of blackened steel tubes launches a brain-wilting barrage of rockets every fifteen minutes or so. I have said this before, but it can be hard to know what you are looking at here, although some elements are familiar. If you served in Vietnam, which I did not, it must feel like the opening of the Tet Offensive in 1968, but with a more benign intent and much better dancing.

Some of these "native" girls are quite fetching, although one or two have suspiciously pale skin, as if perhaps they've been recruited more for their appearance and fluid dance moves than their indigenous heritage. I wonder if they only want to have fun, which it certainly is for both the spectators and the dancers. The exception is our dog, Brownie, who is shuddering now on her well-worn Bacardi beach towel under our dining table. Human religion, of whatever brand or belief system, has never been her thing. She is an unrepentant creature of the earth.

The two dueling steel drummers, both long deaf, I'm sure, although not old, can tell by watching each other's hands and elbows what is happening next. Clearly it's a kind of sign language within a specific culture. After long attendance at those festivals as musicians, husbands and wives must have to yell at each other and the children across the breakfast table every day. But don't we already realize this—that we all must know each other in different ways in order to connect in this town, this country?

The blue and white balloon-covered arches have been

complete and ready for half an hour, wired into place on the posts above the floral standards. Each year the design of the shrine changes, and not by only a little. This is a creative endeavor that brings out the best in its neighborhood builders. Soon the Holy Cross itself, twenty feet long and eight wide at the transverse member (I have seen this ritual six times before), on the shoulders of its patient but honored bearers, will be making its way down from the Cerro de las Cruzes above to this ceremonial apotheosis. As the bearers trudge through it, the destruction of the waiting shrine floor painting will be like an ancient blood offering. It's there for a day, no more, as, in a sense, are we all. For them, this is a moment to live for. At the margins, the gringos are all waiting with their cameras ready, as the locals are with their souls. Somewhere out there in the hills, the cross is already on its way. Soon we will hear the chanting and the cries of people connecting to their roots. The closest thing I can think of to this in the States is the Wave at a World Series game. But that is not religious, you object. I will politely disagree.

Then the costumed dancers begin their rhythmic descent from the hilltop above. Their ankles are wrapped with strings of shells that respond to each move. The Policía Tránsito block the street behind them and they pass through the balloon arches and approach the tinted sawdust sanctuary, where they withdraw to the sides as the cross moves in. It is lowered to touch the ground at the base and rest on an altar at the head. A dozen senior dancers assemble within the arches and begin their ancient moves. The priest awaits them. Who knows what this pattern of tribute once saluted? Like many things here it may be the old adapted to the new, reinforcing both. This country is big on continuity, even if the individual connections from creed to creed are by now somewhat blurred. The main thing is to have one and celebrate it.

Half an hour later an enormous and deafening barrage of rockets soars over our house, and the charred and broken sticks of their tails drop on our courtyard like cinders from a burnt offering. A mixed metaphor indeed, but so is this ceremony. Mexican religion on the whole is a graft of Spanish Catholicism upon the captured but only partially yielding body of indigenous ritual.

For the next few weekends until the end of May it will be repeated, each time with a new set of variations, in a different neighborhood, until no one remains without hearing problems. One is tempted to think that the rockets are provided by the union of San Miguel Otologists, the doctors who treat hearing loss, only there are none here.

It is not like this everywhere. When I was growing up in Minnesota, after the Christmas *lefse*, a Norwegian flatbread, was finished, and then the thaw five months later, we had the smelt run in the north. It may have originated as a ceremony honoring the first living thing that moved in the spring. Although it attracted a crowd that towed boats behind their SUVs, it did not evoke the same range of florid emotion that we have here, even if it furnished many costumes: multi-pocketed vests and waterproof hip boots topped by canvas hats displaying hand-tied flies. While unique and clearly regional, the participants did not have the same color sense, and no one, in my recollection, danced. The passion behind the event, although intense with anticipation and aquavit, was of a less demonstrative, more northern European quality.

I didn't think of this on those occasions, but the Native Americans of that once contested territory were always excluded from this display. They were generally kept in the background the entire year, as if their credentials were in question, and their names mainly appeared on the jerseys of high school and college athletic teams as emblems of bravery.

No pun intended.

These are the rites of spring, no matter where they occur: ceremonies of courting, or of breeding, or of death and rebirth. They reassure us that, despite the clang of cell phones and the bleep of tweeting and texting, we are still part of a long chain of cycles that extends not only back through our own lives, but through those of generations long gone, as well as forward to those yet to be born. They are annually repeated to bind us to our traditions, no matter how tenuous, to connect us to the roots of our culture, to remind us that death is a part of life. They instruct our children in what they will be expected to do in their own time, and what to pass on to their offspring, and theirs in turn.

April, the month of Easter and a variety of other causes to celebrate, also gave us the Good Friday procession on Calle 20 de Enero, where, during my conversation about house inspections with Gordon Logan, my car was nearly frozen in place during the stations of the cross, I believe at the one where Veronica wipes the face of Jesus with her veil. These are all, in a way, public entertainment dressed up as a pious lesson, a formula that has worked for many generations, and still (mostly) works today.

There used to be puppet shows all over México that illustrated, in full costume, the history lessons that had made the country virtuous and free. Designed and presented for illiterate people, they were and still are better for the youth here than video games. At least the stylized violence offered by these historical shows had a purpose.

Although the Santa Cruz procession I have sketched above is local, it occurs in other towns as well. It goes on beyond the tolerance of even the most rabid party animal, and some expats leave for quieter regions during this explosive period. To see a detailed list of other religious ceremonials, many of them more important and elaborate than this one, see the website of Viva San Miguel. You'll find a day-by-day list of fiestas for the entire year. This site is a valuable resource for many activities in this town. From the link below, you can connect to their home page and navigate to your main areas of interest. Look particularly at their heading Links at the top of the page. Paste this into your browser: http://vivasanmiguel. com/festivals_%20fiestas_sma.htm

CHAPTER 11

COMMUNITY

Aside from sharing information on how to change the electric bill into our own name when we buy a house, and where to get good blue cheese, what do we do in San Miguel together? What are the elements that make us part of one group rather than another, or of none? Is being an expat in a Mexican city a barrier to linking up with others, or is it more of a tie that can be helpful and productive? In short, how do we connect with each other, when we do?

México has always been a land of great disparities among people of different social classes. Many observers feel that as the gap in income grows in the U.S., a similar social rift is widening there, even as the middle class is growing here. This is not a promising trend for people in the north. A society that works best is one in which the largest possible number of people is invested in its outcomes. Marginalizing people, whether for reasons of race, gender, religion, or sexual orientation reduces their sense of belonging and undermines their desire to attempt to participate productively in the life of society. They acquire the sense of being pushed away from opportunity in their own lives, from the table of bounty that they see can be so rich for others. A common outcome of this is that they become mere clients of the government, which is often guilty of encouraging dependence out of its desire to grow and increase its own importance.

It is no surprise then, that investment in the San Miguel community is the theme of a wide range of charitable groups here, NGOs as they are often called (non-government organizations). As I mentioned at the opening of this book, the Library, the Biblioteca, has sponsored a house tour every Sunday for many years. The Biblioteca itself is celebrating its sixtieth anniversary as I write this. It is an enormous community resource. Aside from helping with operating expenses, the beneficiaries of the house tour have been a long series of scholarship recipients who have seen their educational qualifications and skill levels lifted enough to reposition them to make a better life for themselves and their families. Many hundreds of these students would never have had the means to continue in school without it.

Public school education is free and compulsory here only through the sixth grade. After that it costs money, fees that, even if not large, are still often beyond the means of poor parents. College costs are partially subsidized, and modest by U.S. standards, but even so, they remain well beyond the reach of large numbers of promising students. For many expatriates looking for a way to make a difference in San Miguel, this presents an open door too inviting to be overlooked.

When I was doing a series of articles on charitable organizations for mexconnect online magazine, one group I came across that seeks to remedy this problem is called Jovenes Adelante. It offers grants for college tuition, provides a laptop, furnishes English tutoring, and holds mentoring sessions on a monthly basis. The majority of the students they assist are women because, ironically, girls can't earn as much as boys of similar age and are therefore more easily spared by their families to continue in school. In this situation the constant gender bias here rebounds to their benefit. Mujeres in

Cambio is another organization that provides scholarships, in this case for young women from the countryside.

Another worthwhile group is Casita Linda. Put quite simply, its task is to construct small houses at no cost for people who don't have one and are not likely to ever be able to put together the resources to build one. These are families often living in improvised shelters made of sheet metal, scrap timbers, cardboard, and advertising banners. They are invited to participate in the construction. Casita Linda's largest model house costs about $8,000 to construct. One condition is that the recipient must own title to the small parcel of land on which it is built. Otherwise the landlord would take it over on completion and eject them, or raise the rent beyond manageable levels. I ran into the former director one recent morning at the Saturday organic market and he told me they had just completed their seventy-eighth house. Imagine the life-changing experience for those seventy-eight families! Every one of their children will grow up differently because of Casita Linda. The opportunities for making a real difference here are always at hand. Nobody in the administration of these organizations is paid a dime (or a peso). By contrast, look up the executive salaries and perks of some of the largest U.S. charities. You will be appalled.

A third San Miguel group is the only Audubon chapter in México, and it's more than forty-five years old. In addition to traditional bird walks, it provides ecological education in the elementary schools in San Miguel, including a series on recycling and one on endangered species.

Here is a list of similar organizations, currently eighty-two, from *Access San Miguel, the* resource to explore in many areas about SMA: http://www.accesssanmiguel.com/category-ngos-and-charities.html

Of course, not every worthy cause is well publicized,

and some can spring from nowhere with catastrophic force and without warning. Some situations are completely individual and local, and life changing beyond belief. The NGOs above are all designed to address problems endemic to the community, issues that, like the poor, are always with us, but when the unexpected happens there are often no organizations ready to help out. What follows then? Here is a painful example that happened to people I know.

Bob Remak and Antonieta Espinosa were married in 2011 here in San Miguel. Bob had come down from Santa Barbara in 2009, and Antonieta was born and raised in San Miguel. When they married, she already had two boys who were twenty-one and sixteen years old, Leonardo and Eduardo. Like so many other expats, they met at a Spanish language school, one that specializes in teaching the language to adult expats and visitors, and in an interesting sidebar, provides a point of connection where numerous newcomers and residents alike can make new and lasting friends. This has happened to us, as well as many other people we know. The difference in this case was that Antonieta was no expat; she was Bob's Spanish teacher.

I pulled up at their house in the La Lejona neighborhood on an unusually gray and drizzly day in May. As I parked the clouds released their burden in an unwelcome rush and I sat behind my streaming windows mentally calculating the distance in inches from my door to theirs. Still, we needed the rain, and some weather turbulence on the Pacific Coast was stirring things up.

The maid let me in. The house is relatively new and opens onto an inviting garden space at the back with a long, modern fountain in the center. A small table held a boxed deck of Uno cards now soaked by the unexpected downpour. In the living room I found a small tabletop altar devoted to a teenage boy. It held childhood photos, mementoes, and a stumpy candle. Religious icons. I couldn't begin to read the connected significance of it all, but it was a hint of what was to come. Five minutes later Bob and Antonieta drove up.

Some people have heard parts of this story as it developed, but I never knew the entire narrative as I was about to hear it. The three of us sat at the dining table. Bob and Antonieta appeared to have braced themselves for this, as I had tried to do myself, but they wanted to tell the story.

"Please tell me what happened from the beginning. How did it start?"

Antonieta began. "On June 9, my sister-in-law came by to tell us that our son Eduardo was in the hospital. Apparently he was hit by a train. One of the first problems we had to deal with was that he was bleeding a lot."

"From a cut to the leg," added Bob. "Let me start again. It was a Sunday and we had dropped him off with some friends earlier that day. He was walking home along the train tracks. There were no witnesses to it except the engineer, so we only have what he said. Eduardo had his back to the train. It came around a blind curve; he couldn't see it. At the turn it was probably 75 to 100 meters from where he was. The engineer saw him, tooted his horn, but he didn't get any reaction from Eduardo."

"Was the boy walking right on the tracks?"

"Yes, with his back to the engine and his headphones in, because they found them connected, and he was also talking on the phone. The person on the phone could hear the train but Eduardo couldn't hear it because of the headphones. From the accident, at the last minute he had to have heard the train, because the impact came on the left arm. His elbow was dislocated, then it collapsed his ribs from that initial impact. Then his head went in and it fractured his skull on the front."

It seemed as if he must have been turning around in

111

the process. "Do you know how fast the train was going then?"

"It couldn't have been going that fast, because it came to a complete stop within about 700 meters. I did some research and it said that a train traveling at 55 miles per hour takes two miles to stop."

"I can believe that." In college I had worked on the railroad one summer and we used to see cars race us at street crossings, as if we could stop on a dime if they came too close. The engineer I always worked with on that night shift had killed nine people in six different accidents over his long career.

"Also, there was one curve they just came out of and they were going into another curve and then the station was coming up, so I'm sure they were slowing down."

Running those numbers I came up with a train speed of about eleven miles an hour. That doesn't sound very fast, but to give this some perspective, if you were running a marathon at an average speed of eleven miles an hour you'd turn in a time of 2:23—not worth an Olympic medal, but quite a respectable time nonetheless. Part of this equation is the sheer mass of a train, compared with the mass of a human body.

"We know that he turned, because the impact came here." Bob placed his palm on his forehead toward the left side. "Also the hit on his legs was well above the knee, where the cowcatcher is. It came halfway up his thigh. They found him on the side of the tracks. The engineer ran back once they stopped the train, and they looked under it, but he was over on the side when the paramedics got there. They realized he had a head injury because of the way he was reacting. He was combative, which they said was normal for head injuries, but they were able to calm him down. At that time they saw the cuts on the legs, and by the time they got to the hospital the bleeding was heavy and that's all they saw. They needed thirteen blood donors just to replace the blood."

One point to take note of here is that people need to provide their own blood donors in México. This issue will carry even more weight in the following chapter, called HEALTHCARE.

"At that moment we didn't know what happened," said Antonieta. "But the first priority was to stop the bleeding. Then they started the first surgery. I can't remember the time. He came out of it at three o'clock in the morning. I signed some papers in case they needed to amputate his leg. I saw his eye. He told us he had a hit in the head. When the X-ray person passed I told her to take some X-rays of his head. She told me no, because the doctor didn't order it. I said that didn't matter, I will pay for that. I want you to do it because he said he has a hit here in the head. And she said no again, that she cannot do it without an order from the doctor."

"The nurse came out at three o'clock," continued Bob, "and said they had stopped the bleeding. This was the start of our roller coaster ride, because six or seven times he was dying, then he was saved, during the course of the following twenty-eight days. We were both very happy, and then at 3:30 in the morning the doctors came out and said they had discovered the fractured cranium. It was life threatening, and at that time they said, 'First of all, we can't do the required surgery here in San Miguel. We don't have the equipment or the neurosurgeon."

"And also," added Antonieta, "they told us that night that his cranium was fractured like a puzzle. It would be almost impossible to put it again together. They needed a specialist, so we were thinking then it would be very hard to save his life."

"They pretty much said that they couldn't save his life then," said Bob. "They could have him transferred to Leon, but because of the bureaucracy in the hospital, and the time and his condition, they said, 'If I were you I would go find a private doctor.'"

"Were you operating under Seguro Popular (a state health insurance system)?"

"No. We had absolutely no insurance. We have it now, but we hadn't signed up yet then. By this time whether we had any insurance or not, this was something that this local hospital couldn't take care of. I mean, even if we had the insurance, they still couldn't have handled it. It's just that the way the hospitals are organized in San Miguel, there is no neurosurgeon or the tools to do that kind of surgery. This was, as I said, at 3:30 in the morning. He had gotten to the hospital at seven o'clock the evening before."

At that time Eduardo's stepmother had been informed of the accident and came up with a neurosurgeon recommendation, and they contacted him. The surgeon appeared at seven o'clock that morning.

"He came," said Antonieta, "and the first thing he did was order him into intensive care. Then he came out and talked with us and said that he can do it. He said he had done many surgeries that were that same situation or worse. And then we needed to think about the money because we didn't have any money at that time. They were talking about it and they told us 250,000 pesos for everything (about $20,000 U.S.)."

"Well," said Bob, "first of all I had closed my business (a burrito restaurant) two months before and I had never been so broke. We had 540 pesos to our names. But we said, yes, of course, let's do it. They then arranged for the ambulance and Eduardo was taken to Querétaro, where he was admitted. I had $5,000 left on my credit card limit and that got him in. Eduardo's father was going to arrange his half, and we had contacted a friend who loaned us some money. Once we got him in, he was put into an induced coma. This is Monday at one o'clock. The surgery was scheduled for the next morning."

"In a couple of days," added Antonieta, "we realized that what the hospital had said was not right."

"They had estimated 50,000 pesos a day for intensive care. But the bill for the first two days was close to 200,000 pesos," said Bob.

"He had the surgery on Tuesday night," she added.

"Which had been delayed because of a lack of blood," Bob continued. "Here you have to provide blood donors, and this was an emergency, so we were trying to get everyone we could, but they're saying, no, you don't have enough blood yet. We can't do the surgery because of that. this actually made no sense to me. It was finally done Tuesday evening and it was a success. The surgeon was able to put a lot of the parts back in, he was very skillful. He also put in three titanium plates, so in the end it was a great success. They also cleaned up his legs because his right leg was just a deep cut, but on the other leg the bone was broken and needed a foot-long pin. So on Tuesday night they had that surgeon come in and he opened that up and cleaned it to try to minimize the chance of infection. Eduardo spent two days coming out of the induced coma. Antonieta went into the room on Thursday and he said, 'Mama.' Friday afternoon he got out of intensive care and we were very happy because the surgery to put the pin in his leg was scheduled for Monday, but then we noticed that he was running a temperature. Over the weekend he had seemed fine. He was coming back and he told me he was having trouble talking. From the hit on the left side of his head his right side had trouble moving—he had very limited movement there. They said that would recover. I asked him how he was doing and he said, 'good, 90%.' Then during that weekend the temperature developed further and the problems with eating started."

It was during this early phase that help from outside started to develop. Antonieta's employers came up with the money for the pin needed for the shattered leg. Others came forward with a variety of efforts. Cousins went to the television and radio stations and posted announcements. Antonieta's sister canvassed the neighborhood and her market. The money deposited at the hospital began to grow.

The original estimate for the care had been 250,000 pesos, a number that was largely, and could only be, a guess. By the time it was finished, the total was 1.5 million pesos. ($120,000 U.S.) The boy's father was able to come up with $12,500. Friends gave Bob and Antonieta personal loans of $10,000.

"One day a lady came to our room with a little card, el Divino Niño (the Christ Child). It's a prayer card," Bob said.

He reached into his wallet and pulled it out. "There's a prayer on the back. We started saying the prayer for Eduardo and it kept working. I'm not much of a believer, but it was working. Meanwhile, Leo (Eduardo's brother) had called and said, 'Do you need anything?'

"I said, 'Yes, can you find someone to loan us $30,000?' He said he had an idea, and twenty minutes later we got a call from one of his childhood friends. He was managing his mother's estate. He said, 'I have $30,000 for you.' We'd also gotten a $1,500 loan from a friend when we needed to buy the pin for the leg. Ten thousand from another friend, and eight thousand from another. People she worked with would come by every once in a while with money. Antonieta's cousin and sister came by with contributions."

At about this time a man came forward who had experience in arranging fundraising events. He knew what to do. They collected a variety of prize donations and sold raffle tickets for 500 pesos, about $39.00. This raised thousands of dollars.

"The thing I really want to say," Bob continued, "is that it was the support of the community, from our friends and family with loans, and the community of San Miguel. Without this support coming in, first of all, how we would've have even eaten in the hospital, how we would have thought we'd be able to pay the bills, I can't imagine. I don't know what would've happened. It filled our hearts with energy, some of which was passed on to Eduardo. It took away some of the preoccupation. He died radiating love, and it wouldn't have been possible without this."

In the course of this ordeal Eduardo had five surgeries over twenty-six days, the last one exploratory to find what the doctors thought was a hole in his stomach, as food was leaking out. On Saturday morning, four weeks after the accident, the doctor informed them that he wasn't going to make it. They could put him on a respirator, but it wouldn't change the outcome. There was no longer any hope, and Eduardo died later that morning.

Silence blanketed the room for a while. Finally I picked up the thread again.

"Has this experience changed your sense of what this community is like?"

"For me, yes," Antonieta said. "Because I was born here and I lived all my life here, but I never saw before how strong our community is, how they can come together for one cause like Eduardo. I think for me it was something I could not believe. The young people, the old people, even the strangers. Some that know us only barely, and some that know us very well. The sense of community was very strong. Now I realize that if we did it for this time, we can also do it for other times for sure."

"Antonieta kept saying in the hospital that she was happy we were here instead of in Santa Barbara when this happened because of the support we were getting. What this did for me was cement the idea that San Miguel was my home. I came down here to learn Spanish, and I ended up marrying my Spanish teacher. It had been home for me for a while, but who knew what the future might be."

"So have you thought," I asked, "about what kind of support you might have gotten in a different community? I know that's hard to define."

"I don't know what would've happened in Santa Barbara if we had been back in the States. There would've been some support, I'm sure, but... One of the things about San Miguel, and one of the reasons we got the support we did is the size that it is. Antonieta was well known in this community. She grew up here, she's taught people for eighteen years, and we also had the restaurant. I was in some ways a public person. I think even for people who didn't necessarily know us directly, there was still a connection. Would that have happened someplace else? I just don't know.

"I also realized when I was doing the letter for a thank you to the community, that for me, when I came here, there was *something* that drew me to San Miguel. It was hard to put into words, but it spoke to my soul. It's difficult to say what that was, but we felt it. The same thing that's attractive in San Miguel that speaks to some people in their souls is what we experienced from the community here."

"I would like to add something; faith," said Antonieta. "Faith is important here, and in the beginning, when we were in the hospital, we needed that faith to keep going. There was the night we received the money for the surgery, or the money so we would keep eating as we waited. It was faith in the Virgin of Guadalupe, faith in the story of the prayer on the small card of the Divino Niño. There was also the story that a small child tried to save Eduardo at the time of the accident. I believe it because Eduardo asked me about the girl. How was the girl? Before that he was thinking about himself. How was the girl? She tried to help me avoid the hit (impact). And I believe it. He described the girl, and I know that this girl exists in some place. We believe it that this happened. The morning that Eduardo passed away, I saw Roberto pray with the Divino Niño. This man came here without faith, and now he has faith in you (el Divino Niño). At the cemetery I realized that we had many miracles. We needed to believe that his life was part of this energy, this universe, and we need to continue with it. Even though it was painful to bury his body, we know that his soul…"

Bob wiped the tears from her face as she spoke.

"He never lost consciousness (aside from the surgeries and the induced coma)," he added, "that first night after the accident. He asked his mother about the little girl. He asked later whether she was about six or seven years old. She had pulled him from the tracks at the last minute.

"There was no little girl," said Bob, with a sigh. "The engineer didn't see her. I came to believe, as much as someone can who is not a believer, that it was an angel. I have a lot of confidence, and we went through a rollercoaster; he's going to die, he's going to be better, no, he's going to die. It happened so many times. I thought to myself, if it *was* an angel, why would an angel come down to save him, only to have him die later? But at the end, it became clear. Those days in the hospital were a blessing. I think Eduardo always knew he was loved, but like all people we have our internal scars. The time in the hospital was a time for healing all that. In his soul, he knew he was loved, and that's a reflection that came from us, but it was supported by this community. One night in the hospital his parents asked for his forgiveness. And he asked them for forgiveness. I felt he had finished what he had come to this earth to do."

ᏜᏜᏜ

Well... I'm not sure what to add to that. Perhaps nothing can be added because it needs nothing more. The hardest task life offers is to bury one's own children. As I write this I can still see Antonieta's coworkers and her support group, wearing shirts saying *Antonieta's Angels*.

To summarize the effects of this disaster: Bob and Antonieta lost one of their children, wound up $50,000 in debt, and gained an entirely different sense of community in San Miguel.

Perhaps because the San Miguel expat community functions at times like a tiny, yet still oddly diverse town within a small, but larger city, it may have been easier to assemble a substantial response to a crisis in a short period of time. Neighbors called neighbors and friends called friends. Since Bob and Antonieta are a mixed American and Mexican couple, the outpouring of support was a bicultural effort in a way that many are not. Family acts as a dynamic in México in ways that it does not in the U.S., simply because the safety net here is narrower and less substantial than in the north. The news hit Facebook, Twitter, and the Civil List. It's hard to make a comparison with what might have happened if this had occurred in an American or Canadian city, and it is not my point to try. This is, in fact, what happened here in a single, vivid instance in the year before I'm writing this, and I present it as a rather unique example, not a standard. Still, it illustrates the kind of energy the community can focus on a single, catastrophic event.

As we look about for a definition of community, we can see it in action in situations like this.

CHAPTER 12

HEALTH CARE

One of the areas of greatest uncertainty for people thinking of settling in San Miguel, or anywhere in México, is the subject of health care. Sooner or later everyone is going to need to use some aspect of this system. Is it any good? Does anyone in that business speak English? Do you have to go back up north for treatment if you have more than a persistent hangnail? Can you get health insurance as an expat living out of your home country? Is Medicare a resource you can use here?

I am not going to attempt to get specific about all the services and personnel available. The website listed below is that of the San Miguel Medical Resource Directory. It will furnish you with a far more complete roster of this field than I could ever do, and it is also updated more often than I could manage if I were to try to do something similar in this book. The version I'm looking at online now was last revised four months ago.

I can't imagine a more complete compendium of local health care information. It includes overviews of nearly every kind of care, language issues, medical records, insurance, emergency numbers, pharmaceuticals, and a nearly endless list that goes on and on. It includes both dentists and holistic practitioners. This is an indispensible aid and it is the resource we use ourselves. As with any site of this kind, check whether the specifics of any single resource are a good fit for you, and that the information is current, before you attempt to use it. http://www.smahealthinfo.com

Spend some time exploring this website and you will get a more detailed idea of what is offered in this town. Check out as well the other websites it lists. Look at the categories titled Seguro Popular and IMSS for information about afford-able government health care programs open to expats who need not have a *permanente* visa status to use it. Bear in mind that coverage of this type is not complete, and some things they cover are not available in San Miguel. For example, in the case of a heart attack, they do not cover the coronary artery stents.

For Americans residing abroad, one of the unfortu-nate provisions of the Medicare program in the United States is that you cannot use its benefits outside the U.S. after you been gone more than sixty days. I won't speculate on the rea-sons why, but they must partly have something to do with the difficulty of verifying claims and charges, the potential for fraud, and certifying the credentials of practitioners and in-stitutions. I'm sure there are other reasons, and I won't try to judge their validity. It is what it is, and while I know there are a few people in Congress trying to change these rules, I do not expect any outcome from that effort soon, if ever.

The Canadian health care system also has residency requirements, but will in some cases reimburse the patient.

Because my experience suggests that personal anecdote is often more revealing in ways that lists or data-bases, as valuable as they are, can never be, I recently had a conversation with Wendy Weber, a woman who moved down here from Kansas City with her husband, Jim Knoch, a few years ago. I was startled to discover that she had just had hip replacement surgery, and I was eager to speak with her about her experience using the Mexican medical system. I've known Wendy for a number of years and she is both frank and articulate.

I visited with her at her home on a quiet street in the San Antonio neighborhood.

In one sense a hip replacement is an elective procedure, because you're not going to the hospital by ambulance and it's not an emergency. But at the same time it's more serious than many other procedures, and I would have to consider it major in nearly every way, even if it falls somewhat short of heart valve replacement or brain surgery. Mobility is a critical issue for all of us. Even if we're at an age when we don't get around as fast or as much as we used to, we still do like to get around.

Wendy and I settled into a small courtyard. I could hear the bleating of a baby goat somewhere over the wall. I didn't want to think about why it was there. A favorite dish in the neighboring state of Jalisco is *birria*, a goat stew.

"Tell me about your recent decision to have your hip replacement done in México. Was there a choice between doing it here or doing it in the States?"

"I went to Doctor Michael Schmidt in Querétaro because of his reputation, just to have my knee X-rayed. I've had several knee surgeries since the sixties. I told him, 'and while you're at it, why don't you X-ray my hips?'

"When he had finished he said, 'you know the bad news is that your knee is really bad. You've had no cartilage there forever. The *very* bad news is that you have advanced osteoarthritis in your hip, probably caused by that knee, and you need to have the hip replaced.'

"He suggested I go back to the States and talk to some doctors there to get a second opinion, and to check out the Medicare benefit. I have no insurance other than Medicare

(Wendy is a young 66) and so I then researched the costs. The range in the States for a hip replacement was from $40,000 to $140,000. I talked to him (Dr. Schmidt) about the price here and what I liked about his price was that it was all-inclusive. Everything: the pre-surgery process, the follow up meetings, the hospital."

"How much was that going to come to here if Dr. Schmidt did it?"

"He said it would be 175,000 pesos, which is what..." (using the exchange rate I was getting during that time period, 12.8 pesos per dollar, that was $13,672.) "I got a second opinion, which said exactly what Dr. Schmidt had said. I've talked to a lot of people over the years in the States. We don't have a home up there anymore, so we would've had to go up and stay there, find someone to stay in our house here, and take care of five animals. I didn't want to do that; I wanted to be here at home. Dr. Schmidt has an excellent reputation. Jim and I both met with him three times before we made the decision, and we decided to go ahead. I've been malpracticed upon so many times in the States with this knee, and that's what started this whole problem with my hip."

"Was Dr. Schmidt trained in the U.S.?"

"He's German and Italian, so I think he did that in Europe. He's been here sixteen years. He has his own clinic with four rooms, so it's not a big hospital. You're not going to end up with some terrible disease just from being in a hospital."

"You mean it was done in a *clinic*?" Initially I found this startling, but in thinking about it for a minute, why not? As I was to discover, the threat of getting a hospital-based infection was always at the back of Wendy's mind, and I think that a patient's attitude going in for surgery can have some influence on the outcome.

"It was done in *his* clinic. Upstairs he has four rooms, with an operating room. It's beautiful, it's clean, they cater the food, too much food, really, and it was lovely. The nurses are lovely too. It was great. He's there, he's around all the time. There are three, or maybe four doctors working there. They do everything from emergencies to spines, knees, hips, boobs and liposuction. I don't know which one does the last two; but he doesn't."

"Would you call him an orthopedic surgeon?"

"Orthopedic surgeon and traumatologist. He's done thirty years worth of hips and knees."

"How long did you stay in the clinic?"

"Four days. That's what he said it would be, and that's what it was." The tone in which she said this expressed her ongoing trust.

"You stayed in a room in that same building?"

"Upstairs in that same building. They used a spinal block instead of general anesthesia, which is wonderful."

"So the recovery is a whole lot easier."

"Oh, yes. I had my fist in the air saying 'hi' to Jim when I came out of surgery. I couldn't believe it. The room where I stayed is big; it had a place where Jim could stay the night if he wanted to. There was a nice big bathroom and a large window."

It is customary in México for a family member to stay with the patient overnight.

"So you had really done your research before this process began."

"I did a lot of research online with knee doctors in the States, because I knew that eventually I'd have to have my knee replaced. I just didn't realize at that point that my hip would have to be done first."

"You said the range was $40,000 to $140,000 in the

United States."

"Yes, it was all over the place, state by state, and Medicare pays around $11,000 to $12,000 of it, so I guess if you can find a doctor to do it for $12,000, you'd be covered, but that didn't seem very appealing to me."

"That's all Medicare will pay on it?"

I knew that the tone of my voice was one of dismay more than anything else. What good, I thought, was Medicare, if you had to use a veterinarian for your surgery, just to get it fully covered? Wendy was nodding vigorously.

"Yes, and I was shocked too. At least that's what I read, and I've heard different stories from different people, people who have full insurance and a place to live when they go back to the States. And I know a lot of people who've had it done here, by a variety of doctors."

"This is starting to sound like a no-brainer."

"That's what I thought too. Plus, you're at home. When you leave the clinic you're coming directly home."

"To your own bed, which is a comfort, not in some cheap motel on the outskirts of a town you don't know."

"Exactly, or in a rehab facility. Now, here there's no physical therapy for hips. For knees, there's a bunch."

"So your current task is to wean yourself from those crutches." A pair was draped across the sofa where she sat.

"Right, and I go back to see Dr. Schmidt every two weeks. The next visit will be tomorrow, so it will have been four weeks, and if anything, I'll have a cane by then."

"Having made that choice, partly for reasons of affordability, and partly for reasons of confidence in Dr. Schmidt, how would you rate this experience in terms of the overall quality of the care?"

"The quality of care was excellent. The nurses were nice. I asked them what they would do if someone comes in who doesn't speak Spanish, because I do. They said, 'We use hand signals,' and of course, Dr. Schmidt is multi-lingual.' "

Without success, I was trying to imagine which hand signals would be required for some specific needs. Best to get a spouse or friend to stay with you if your Spanish is faulty. Considering the cost level involved, you could hire a translator to come in at key points.

"I thought the experience overall was excellent, although I had a terrible reaction to the tape, of all things, the one they used on the bandages. To me, it was like poison ivy. I called him and he said, 'come on in here tomorrow morning.' He's available all the time. No pain, by the way, although there was plenty of pain medication. There was any kind of pain remedy I would've needed. I had one of those bulbs you can squeeze, I guess it had morphine in it. I left it turned off, not even knowing what it was. I didn't need it. I've had no pain since, but for some itching."

"Do you think the clinic staff there has a different attitude toward patients than what you experienced in the U.S. during hospital visits there?"

"I certainly think there's a different attitude with doctors and their patients, and with nurses too. They both will spend time with you, they will push you to ask questions, to the point where I didn't know what to ask anymore. They're extremely caring and they'll go out of their way to make sure things are all right. I found they didn't have that time pressure issue that the doctors did in the States, that 'fifteen minutes and you're out' system. The doctor was always asking. 'Any more questions?'"

"Have you had any hospital experiences in the United States to compare this with?"

"My first hospital experience up there was when a doctor operated on the wrong side of my knee, which was what led to all these other problems. I used to dread going to the doctor and I hated hospitals. Even visiting someone, I always felt like I was going to get sick. Here the clinic was small and immaculately clean."

"Would you have been as ready to do this operation here if your Spanish was not what it is?"

"That's a good question, and I think I would've, because of Dr. Schmidt speaking English. Jim had earlier spent a night in the heart hospital in Querétaro. I was with him, and I'm happy that I was, because he had a hard time knowing who was coming in to take a food order, versus who was coming to clean the floor. But in this little hospital, even the person who came in four times a day to clean the room, if I asked her for a bottle of water, immediately she went after it. I know some people who say, when I go to the doctor I want them to speak English, and I agree, because, even though I know Spanish, I want to be sure I understand."

"Because there are a lot of specialized terms. What would you say to a person who's considering having surgery done in México?"

"Great! Do it, and do it with confidence. But just like you would do in the States, pick your doctors carefully, get recommendations, and don't use someone who's only done that operation four times. From here to Guadalajara, to Querétaro and México City, all around us there are wonderful specialists in everything."

"Is there anything you would have done differently this time?"

"I don't know what it would have been. Maybe I would have had Jim spend the night that first night in my room."

"Which is customary, isn't it?"

"He could have, but with four dogs and a cat at

home… But, altogether it was the best experience I could imagine."

Once again, a single person's case doesn't make a medical record, whether of one patient, or even less, of an entire local healthcare system. But I wanted to offer this example, which came up as a surprise when I was planning what to put in this chapter, and it was not selected with any foreknowledge as to her outcome when I asked Wendy if she would participate. It was random in that sense. So we cannot generalize from her hip replacement and we won't try. This is mainly an illustration of one woman's experience here when she was faced with limited choices and a very finite budget. With her hip function eroding quickly, could she find a set of options that worked for her? What I like about this example is that she has a number of similar experiences in the United States to compare it with. She may have easily found a venue in the States to have it done, but how then to pay for the shortfall between its actual cost and the Medicare benefit? She was already skittish about U.S. hospital healthcare because of infection risks that she had experienced first hand. These examples can be helpful as we consider whether living in San Miguel would make sense for us in a variety of needs and circumstances.

We have already seen another healthcare example in this book in the chapter just before this one, titled COMMUNITY, where the situation was a dire emergency.

In search of a more general overview of the healthcare climate we live in, I went to see Dr. Roberto Maxwell. Instead of sitting down in his offices on Insurgentes, just down the block from the *biblioteca*, we adjourned to a coffee shop on the plaza on a Saturday morning. Maxwell was trained in México City, and went on to do fellowships in cardiology, pulmonology, and critical care medicine at the University of California, San Diego. He continues to see a GP's group of patients here because this town is too small to support an exclusively specialized practice, although his specialized skills often come into play.

Roberto Maxwell is a man of fifty-seven whose father is American and his mother Mexican. His hair is graying, and at six-foot-two with blue eyes, the Mexican side of his parentage is not at first obvious. He has a friendly, but no nonsense manner. In the conversation that followed I found him refreshingly frank and open. We sat outside in the courtyard over *café americano*, and I asked him about the facilities in San Miguel as he ate a muffin.

"What do we have for a heart hospital here? With so many retired people, that seems like a good resource to have."

"Nothing. We don't have a coronary unit. We do have a three bed intensive care unit at Tec-100 (one of two hospitals here) with heart monitors and a defibrillator, so whenever I have a critically ill patient with a heart attack, or with an arrhythmia or a heart block, I stabilize them at Tec-100 and then if they agree and have the capacity to pay for the angiogram and stents, I take them to Querétaro in an ambulance." (Fifty kilometers away on a good highway.)

"What do we have for a regional trauma center?"

"We don't have one. Here in México, and in San Miguel, all the patients who have trauma and are picked up by the Red Cross, equivalent to a 911 call, they have to be taken to the Hospital General (the government hospital) by law, unless that patient or a family member asks that they be taken to a private hospital."

"Are the Red Cross ambulance crews well trained?"

"All the personnel in the ambulances are trained paramedics, and to be that here you have to take a course (there are three levels) and they need to have passed at least grade one. You cannot be in an ambulance if you're not a paramedic. What we are trying to do now is to pay them well and professionalize them."

"What is the cost of being picked up by an ambulance?"

"If it's an emergency, zero. If you are at the Hospital General and you want to be taken to Querétaro for surgery, then they will charge you. Otherwise, 95% of the work of the Red Cross is free. We're talking about 400 services a month. We have enough personnel for more than three vehicles, but the problem is paying them."

"Could you explain what are the main differences between that Hospital General, and Tec 100?"

Dr. Maxwell explained that Tec 100 is a successful private hospital in Querétaro that rented and refurbished an older but still modern private hospital in San Miguel, one that was formerly called Hospital de la Fe. Then Tec 100 was bought by another group, a conglomerate with interests in other industries as well.

"There are many important differences between Tec 100 and Hospital General. The latter is funded by the government. It's a wonderful hospital physically. Tec 100 is private. To me the most important differences are that in Tec 100 you get admitted by your personal physician, who is the doctor of your choice, and he is responsible for what happens to you and for calling in consultations with other specialists. In Hospital General, you arrive there, and you're seen by one doctor (usually a GP) in the emergency room. Depending on what your needs are, after getting admitted, you will have one doctor in the morning, one in the afternoon, and another doctor in the evening. There may also be different doctors on weekends or holidays. So these doctors are really not responsible for your care, more than on the shift they work in the hospital."

"They don't know you, and continuity in treatment is a big issue."

"Not only that. You have a patient with pneumonia, and they give him two antibiotics in the morning. The doctor in the afternoon comes in and he doesn't agree with those antibiotics, so he changes them. Then the night doctor doesn't like those and he changes them again. Then I come in to make the rounds and I erase all of that and start again. And of course, nobody is responsible. The system is responsible. That to me is a big issue. Another big difference is that very few people in that hospital speak English. I've had a couple of cases in which patients arrive there unconscious. They cannot sign a consent form, so the hospital staff doesn't do many things for the patient (that they might). I've had patients where the family decided, well my dad has had two strokes and he has no quality of life, let him just die. The protocol there is that if you don't have a registered advance directive with them, then they have to follow the protocol."

Which may reflect government or hospital policy more than the informal instructions of the family in the absence of an official advance directive. In some cases this may even mean resuscitating a patient in cardiac arrest, even when he is clearly dying.

"For you personally, in your practice, what do you mean by the phrase *assist someone to die with dignity*?"

"Palliative sedation, which is legal in the state of Guanajuato." Maxwell showed no hesitation in this response. It made me suddenly realize that this man had dealt with *everything*, and was likely to just answer these questions straight out. The greatest fear of the rest of us was *his* daily routine. It took me a moment to digest this. I don't go to doctors any more than anyone else does who is not a hypochondriac.

"So under this sedation he would just drift away. Maybe his departure is partly caused by this sedation. I want to be clear about this."

"You want to let whatever disease the patient has take its course. You will not give him medicine to cure him. You will not take him to surgery or give him antibiotics. You will let the illness take its course and in the meantime keep him very comfortable, and keep him asleep so that the patient will die without pain, with no shortness of breath, no nausea, no coughing."

Dr. Maxwell went on to describe the typical wait times at the Hospital General, which can often be three to four hours in the emergency room, and two to three months for an outpatient visit.

"Are the people using the Hospital General those who have IMSS or Seguro Popular? (both inexpensive government insurance programs.)"

"Anybody can go to Hospital General. Many who have IMSS go to the General anyway, and the Seguro Popular doesn't cover everything. A lot of my patients will ask me if they should buy Seguro Popular or IMSS? I usually tell them, don't buy anything. You can still go to Hospital General and it will be very inexpensive. It is a second level hospital. If you come in with a heart attack, there's no cardiologist. I tell my patients it's a wonderful hospital for those who don't have any other option." His face displayed no irony at this response.

"Do you see people with Seguro Popular going to Clinica Tec 100?"

"Yes, but they will still have to pay, unless they have private health insurance."

"How does the blood bank system here function in emergencies?" I asked this to get more detail on the startling situation Bob and Antonieta had found themselves in with no warning.

"In México it is illegal to buy or sell blood products. If you need blood you have to provide donors. Your group of friends is going to be more or less your age. There comes a problem then with the expat community, since most of them are over sixty-five. Some of the regulations to be a donor are that you have to be eighteen or above, but less than fifty-five. You have to weigh more than fifty kilos, you cannot have tattoos, you can't be a diabetic, or have high blood pressure, or have had hepatitis, HIV, or other contagious diseases. But the real problem is that there is no blood bank here in San Miguel. So what happens when you arrive at Tec 100 with an upper GI bleed, is that I'm going to ask you for a donor. If it turns out you don't know anybody who's eligible to be a donor, the hospital blood bank in Querétaro will ask for a deposit, which is legal because you are not actually buying blood. That's the only way that it works. They'll send the order to Querétaro."

"And then you replace it later."

"Yes, if you want your money back."

"So what happens if I'm in a serious car accident? I'm bleeding profusely and I need surgery immediately."

"You are taken to surgery with no blood as you wait for it to arrive, which might take three or four hours. I've had to give my own blood at times like that."

"I have heard that sometimes the ambulance crew will give it."

"Yes, or the police, whenever we need donors fast. Now that we have Tec 100 it's easier because they do have their own blood bank in Querétaro. In Hospital General they don't have a blood bank, but they do have a reserve of a few units of blood of various types. But in private practice, I don't have access to that."

"Would you say that this blood bank system is one

that could use some reform?" I said this in my most neutral tone of voice. I didn't come down here to be a critic of existing systems but to live within their limits. This was one of the tougher limits.

"I have no doubt. There are people who've had some experiences with this system and they've tried to open a blood bank here. But the first thing Mexican law will require is a hematologist. Where would you find one here in San Miguel? And then of course they require a certain amount of square meters, a freezer, and there's no way a blood bank will survive here economically, as a business."

A lot of this was merely that San Miguel is not a large enough town to support some of the more sophisticated resources people would commonly need. This is not specific to the Mexican health care system.

"Is there a particular lab you favor here?"

"No, there are labs that are cheaper or more expensive. Cheaper does not necessarily mean worse or better. The cheaper ones will seldom email you the results."

Turn around time is another feature that distinguishes among them. Smaller labs often will have to send some things out, so using the cheapest one may be a foolish economy if there is any urgency in your tests.

"Are there home healthcare aides available here?"

"Not such a thing officially. What I do is whenever I have a patient that requires home care I ask around with the nurses at the hospital and see who's willing to do an extra shift with pay." Another workaround, but that is how many things are done, and often done quite well here.

"Now that Hospice San Miguel has closed, what options are there for end of life care?"

"There are only a few doctors in town that know what hospice is and much less have knowledge of hospice care. So my recommendation is that before you get to an end of life situation, shop around the doctors in town and check which one would like to take care of you in that condition. Not all doctors will want to because you get into problems like ethics, religion, and economics. If you have, for example, an advance directive, my preference is to do the terminal phase in the hospital. If you want to do it at Hospital General, you have to have the advance directives notarized, in Spanish with two witnesses, and you have to go out of town and get a stamp so that they register your legal wishes."

"But that is not the case at Tec 100?"

"Well, in that case it's not a hospital responsibility, it's mine. If you have a set of directives that was signed in the States, or if you give me one that is signed by you, I'll respect your wishes."

It was clear to me that this level of informality could not exist in another country to the north where you could be sued for almost anything. Good faith still matters here.

"In your practice do you take medical insurance?"

"No. And the reason is that if you have Mexican medical insurance they'll pay the hospital bills, but they would pay very little to the doctor. If I have a patient in the intensive care unit, the insurance will pay me 400 to 800 pesos a day ($32.00 to $64.00 U.S.). I charge 500 pesos for an office visit. Most of the time what I do is work out a deal where the patient pays me and I'll give him the itemized bill so he can go to his insurance for reimbursement. It may take some time.

"Seventy percent of my patients are expats, Canadian, Americans, or Europeans. In the U.S. they are used to not paying. Everything is picked up by the insurance. I have many patients who come in for the first time and then they just walk out of my office without paying."

"Thinking it'll be somehow taken care of."

"Yes, but we don't even work with those insurance companies. The same thing happens with the hospital. You get admitted and they will require a deposit, a credit card or cash, and then after a week, and you're free to go home or you die, then who pays the bill?"

"So you're probably not up to speed on health insurance for expats living here."

"You can buy Mexican insurance. There is one special program from England for those sixty-five and over, less than eighty-five, and they don't look at your health history. I know that after sixty-five your premiums will go sky-high, paying amounts similar to what you're paying in the States. If $800 a month is not a problem, then I would recommend buying, not Mexican insurance, but international insurance if you're going to be traveling. Another way to see it is that at $800 a month, in three or four years, you could have more then $30,000 in your pocket. Why buy any insurance? Ten thousand dollars here in México will pay a lot of medical bills."

"So you really believe a plausible plan would be to just forget about health insurance."

This so contradicted everything I had learned living most of my life in the States, I could hardly believe it.

"Yes, and of course, people who ask me if they need to buy air evacuation, I tell them not necessarily. When I arrived here almost thirty years ago I would be flying two or three patients per month to the U.S. in air evacuations. I became an air ambulance physician. The medical facilities were very basic then. Now I send only around one patient a year to the U.S."

"You see people that you can help easily, and others that no one can help, so how do you maintain your optimism in this job? Too often you have no control over the outcome of your efforts."

"In my practice? I have a passion for what I do; I like it. I know that I can influence the health of people either in a preventive way, or then curative, and if I cannot prevent it or cure it, then I try to get the right doctor/specialist for them. If they have a set of advance directives saying that they don't want more curative things done for them, then I hope I can help them go in a dignified way, with no pain, no shortness of breath, just to let them go the way I would like to go myself." This question did not fence him in because he saw a positive role for himself in every outcome.

"What health care advice would you give to an expat about to move here?"

"The first thing that I would advise is to find a doctor when you arrive. Please don't wait until you have an emergency. Shop around with three or four doctors who speak the language, that are open to talking with your doctors in the States, ones that keep records. Check their credentials and ask what hospital they use locally or out of San Miguel. Ask them whether if something happens to you will they see you at any hour of the day or night, weekends or holidays. Ask them if there's something they cannot resolve, like a surgical or heart problem, what happens then? Are they going to call another doctor, or are you going to have to come up with one? (In your condition.) When there are things that cannot be taken care of locally, what will he do? We have referrals to Querétaro, Celaya, México City, to Houston. Would he go with you and take care of you there, or is he going to refer you to somebody you don't even know?"

As part of this process, take your Canadian or American paperwork in hand and go into the office of your doctor of choice and set up your records. Become a patient ahead of the need. This way you already have a relationship with that doctor in the case of an emergency. This puts you on the proper path from step one.

"Another thing I would advise is to walk through the hospitals. Get familiar with their facilities, because when you're in the emergency room you can't think about it. Ask your new doctor, if you are in an emergency, who should you call? If you call the ambulance, which one? Get the phone numbers of the services. Get a good address for yourself (one that won't leave the ambulance driver guessing). Decide how you will reimburse your doctor and pay the hospital. Bring your records from the U.S.—the last labs, the last EKG, the last chest X-ray or surgery. Many expats will have a full physical before they come to San Miguel. Bring those records. I think the most important thing is to know who you're going to call when you have an emergency. If you're going to Tec 100 don't arrive without a doctor. Always know who you are going to be seeing there. Even if the initial treatment is done by the ER staff, the emergency room doctors are all GPs. They can do the basics, start an IV, increase your blood pressure while your doctor is on his way.

"There are many doctors who will not show up in the middle of the night, or on the weekends. They will send a GP and connect with him by phone. Then they will still charge you as if they had seen you themselves."

If this is not a complete portrait of the system here in San Miguel, it certainly hits most of the important points. Dr. Maxwell was remarkably relaxed and forthcoming in this conversation, and I learned far more than I ever imagined. Whatever is lacking in this picture, the key strategies for survival are here.

The Mexican health care system as it exists in San Miguel is certainly different from those in the U.S. and

Canada. It is not, however, inscrutable, and it can be navigated with nothing more than a little money, some advance preparation, and considerable common sense. The critical factor is to get connected with it in advance of need by choosing a doctor, to have a plan to follow in the event of a medical emergency, and have the contact information printed out in good-size type and posted at your phone. Included should be some financial information about what credit card to use for admission to a hospital, in case you are not able to state that yourself.

CHAPTER 13

PUBLIC SAFETY

I was sitting in a café beside the *jardín* this morning with my feet up, reading an American newspaper that a friend had brought down and passed along to me. Page one of the travel section had a story that described how everything in México is now the color red: the sky, the soil, all the people and the animals, the buildings and the plants. Better not go down there, it said. Red can be dangerous to your health, since it can whip up people's passions. Isn't that also the color of the bullfighter's cape, or of blood? While there are some shades of difference, it noted, as you would expect, they all fall within a narrow but nevertheless threatening range; it's still all shades of red—pink through burgundy.

This seemed more than a little strange to me, but I don't encounter the American media here that much, and it used to be a reputable newspaper, at one time anyway. I couldn't help covertly looking up to study the scene around me. Not only was everything not red, but *nothing* was red, not a single thing in view. Even those things you'd normally expect to be red weren't. What was going on? I checked the date on the paper and it was not from April 1. Somehow, I thought, Americans who read these newspapers are getting different information about México than what I'm getting as I live here.

Of course this is no more than a bit of hyperbole,

perhaps even of outright fiction. But the point is that I live in a world where the American press and television media constantly describe the reality of crime in México in one way, while my everyday experience here is entirely different, and I mean *entirely* different. There is no common ground, no overlap. How to reconcile these two versions of reality? I could simply say that I *live* here in San Miguel de Allende, and the people who write these stories live somewhere else, perhaps in New York or California, neither of which is without its own filters of reality, so that's enough said. But it isn't, because the press, through constant repetition and exaggeration has had a serious impact on the way many or even most Americans now view México. As I have said in the past, you can't always find the truth in nonfiction, which is what journalism would like to be thought of.

Public safety is an issue almost certain to start a fight, and I knew before I began this book that this chapter would be the hardest one to write. I have already discarded one version of it and started over. The subject of the crime rate in México is the one I most often encounter talking to people who don't live here. I see my obligation clearly: it is to give my reader the most accurate sense that I can of what is going on here on the ground in San Miguel. In the United States, crime varies widely by location, as it does here. No matter which country we reside in, our greatest concern is always going to be about the specific area where we live.

Yet the subject reminds me slightly of the murky clouds surrounding global warming; it's been so politicized that it's difficult to see any of it clearly, whether we're looking at the parts or the whole.

So let me start with this. After living here for the better part of a decade, and traveling extensively all around this country except for Chiapas, Tabasco, and the upper border states, I can say with certainty that the general impression advocated by most of the U.S. media is utterly false, and I find it distressing that so many people have come to believe it simply because of its constant repetition. There are a few articles published in the States from time to time that are accurate and revealing, but they are by far in the minority.

I am no fan of politics on either side of this issue, and to frame the debate within those constraints is to put on blinders. But because I can't write about living in México, or San Miguel, without taking this subject on, here it is, no holds barred, and in the spirit of this book, straight up.

None of us are *ever* fully safe. Every rational adult in every country on earth knows this. Every child knows it better. We have locks on our doors and windows. We copyright our books. If safety were the principal goal in life, we would all live in a tiny walled town near the Canadian border in Idaho.

The task here, whether in business, marriage, parenting, investing, the arts, or merely in living a rewarding life, is to attempt to measure risk against those rewards, and then make reasonable choices. If you select a street corner in downtown Ciudad Juárez as the location to launch your freelance cocaine retailing operation, you had better make sure you schedule a large markup from wholesale, because the length of time you'll have to make a return on your investment will be severely limited. Risk management is always part of the equation here, as it is everywhere. I have often told people that we who live in México respond to the threat of crime just as they do in the U.S.—we identify the hot spots and we avoid them. It's not rocket science, and that's a statement you will never encounter in the U.S. press.

The issue of crime in México falls into two parts. One has to do with the wholesale drug trade, and that gets far more publicity in the United States than the second kind, which is comprised of common muggings, home invasions, and the occasional murder, rape, or purse snatching. Typically the U.S. media lumps all of these together and trumpets the combined total.

Although they are essentially *business crimes*, like the bootlegging murders in Prohibition Era Chicago, the drug trade murders are flashy and spectacular, as they are intended to be. They are chiefly about territory and power, and the press on both sides of the border contributes to the publicity effect of these crimes by dutifully broadcasting them in gory detail. Repeating them often gives the impression that there are more of them than there really are. The tone and shrillness of the American headlines tend to ignore the fact that the majority of the customers that support this drug trade are themselves Americans living within their own borders and buying their drugs much further down the distribution channels at the retail level. You will never see the U.S. media take on this aspect of the issue because their agenda has always been to place all responsibility firmly on México's doorstep.

In México these crimes almost never involve the typical expat, who is rarely interested in the drugs he can't obtain at his local pharmacy. It is neither valid nor helpful to attempt to erect some parallel between these narcotics distribution wars and the everyday existence of people moving here to start a different kind of life than the one they had at home, where they had no thought of scoring big bags of cocaine or heroin either.

The State Department warnings are designed to advise people where murders are geographically concentrated in México. They don't address whether uninvolved passers-by are really at risk. Perhaps they are if a shot goes wild. My sense of this is that the cartels prefer to avoid harming expats if they can. They are, after all, rarely involved in the drug trade beyond buying a nickel bag or two of grass, so they pose no competition in the realm of wholesale distribution. In general, I avoid the border areas too, but many in San Miguel do not, driving back and forth across the line with their eyes and ears open, but generally without incident.

The other kind of crime, what I think of as the typical variety that any city has, ought to be the focus of our concern when we think about our own exposure as expats. How bad is it in San Miguel? One of the problems in assessing this is to separate, for example, cartel-related murders from all other murders in México. I don't know of any statistics that can do this, but if we look at it in terms of Americans murdered in México in a given year, and compare that with similar statistics in the north, we can see that any of us is much more likely to be murdered in some of the major cities in the United States. This does not mean we ought to be complacent about these routine crimes here, just as we should not be complacent about them in the States either, or anywhere. But if safety is your primary concern, or at least a major one, then it is a plausible argument to flee some of the riskier population areas of the United States, not to stay there. We will see further on that riskier does not always mean the larger cities.

There is always the temptation to view these issues personally, and I'm not immune to that. In all the years I've lived here I haven't been the victim of any crimes, nor have I witnessed any. We are out and about at all hours. I travel throughout México frequently for my book projects, even in Michoacán recently, where on my three separate visits within a six-month period, I saw no problems at all. What can I generalize from this? Not much. This sample is only the experience of one person. It does establish, however, that it's possible to live in and to travel outward from an urban setting in México over a years-long time frame and never witness or experience a crime. Trouble spots are those areas that experience statistically more trouble than other places, but they do not exhibit continuous, wall-to-wall trouble. Crime is not like carpeting, its concentrations are full of gaps and peaceful exceptions.

Of course, problems do exist here in San Miguel, and I do know a few people who've had some trouble with break-ins or muggings. One friend had his car stolen, just as I did once in Minneapolis. Knowing what was coming, I prayed that it would never be recovered, but it was, and in a condition that I didn't care to look at. The real question here is to determine whether these risks exceed those in the U.S., and whether they ought to be a factor in your decision to move to San Miguel or not. Specifically, in the ranking of the occurrences of those crimes, where does this town stand?

To gain a better understanding of our position relative to the U.S. and the rest of México, I decided to talk with David Bossman, who's been active with a citizens' organization called San Miguelenses Unidos (San Miguel Residents United) since its founding. Here is a clip from their policy statement: "Working together with the Policía Preventiva and the municipal authorities, SMU will continue to encourage and educate all interested people about ways to take better care of themselves in their homes and on the street. We will continue to develop and share better strategies to protect our families and homes."

David has been a resident of San Miguel for quite some time, much longer than I have. I got to know him as a member of Rotary when I first addressed one of their meetings three or four years ago. He's one of San Miguel's more prominent expat citizens. He is by nature an activist in this or any community he's lived in.

"Tell me about your organization," I said. We were sitting at a painted cast iron table in his back garden in the southeastern corner of town. David is almost a neighbor of mine.

"It was founded in October of 2013 in reaction to what we saw as an increasing level of local crime. This is a successor organization to one that was called the Municipal Security Committee. Then it only focused on expats. Our vision for San Miguelenses Unidos is much wider, going on the theory that we could not be successful in dealing with crime unless the Mexican community took part as well. So what we have now is more than seventy expats and Mexicans involved, (the latter make up about one third of the group), who are directly engaged in making policy and dealing with the local authorities—with a greater or lesser amount of success. We also have a Facebook page called *More Security in San Miguel*, which now has almost 3000 followers. Interestingly enough, I should mention that our Facebook page traffic is two-thirds Mexican. Nearly all of them are from this area, and we have focused that page only on México, mostly on the San Miguel region. We have about 300 of them coming out of México City and 200 out of Querétaro."

David Bossman is a trim man of about seventy with hair buzzed close to the skin. That his soft-spoken manner and unemphatic delivery easily commands attention suggests his long experience with addressing committees and organizations. It could well be the voice of a teacher or a negotiator, seeking a solution beneficial on both sides of an issue, one that can be lived with.

"How does SMU connect with the city government?"

"Not officially." Here David shrugged, and he has the Mexican version of that gesture down almost perfectly. "We'd like to, but we don't yet have official regular meetings with them. We have requested meetings, and we've met with the equivalent of the assistant D.A. He was very welcoming and took many of our questions. The meeting lasted about an hour and a half. The main thing we got out of it is that we have now guaranteed the legal right of every person who makes a criminal complaint, a *denuncia*, to get a copy of their report. Before this, expats were not given a copy. That was very unfair because they went in within twenty-four hours of the event (as is required to file a complaint), signed a piece of paper and never saw it again." The effect of this was that it always looked like a dead end to the victim and made it difficult to check on the status of an investigation without a case to reference.

"Other than this, and I can see that most of your time has been spent with organizational matters and gaining recognition in this early phase, what has the group accomplished so far?"

"We have no doubt whatever—and saying this, we're not looking for credit—that the two meetings Mayor Mauricio Trejo called were in direct response to our calls for more transparency. As a matter fact, he asked me personally to invite members of our group to a formal security meeting, and twenty of our members were invited."

One of the issues the mayor has been concerned about is that often when young men are arrested they're out on the streets again within two days. The criminal code was recently changed so that people are now presumed innocent when arrested. Formerly they were presumed guilty, so it was easier to hold them.

"We were in complete agreement with him on that concern."

"You talked before about an increase in local crime that stimulated the formation of this group. Can you quantify that? People reading this are going to say, well, I know what the crime numbers were here in Albany last year, but how do they compare to San Miguel? Will I be safer there than I am at home?"

"Yes, we have numbers based on the federal statistics. What we found out was that those numbers were more astonishing than we expected. Between the years of 2012 and 2013, and these are the official federal stats they get from the Ministerio Publico (assembled from each state), we found that the principal crimes that were on the increase were house burglaries with violence (home invasions), burglaries themselves, rape, and auto thefts. In those categories, the rate went up year over year by 22%. That's an enormous increase. Rape was particularly startling, looking at it only against the local areas, like Leon, we had officially twenty-five rapes per 100,000. Leon, to give you a perspective, had about twelve. It's more than double that here."

Leon has a population of about one and a half million.

"In terms of homicide," David continued, "in the State of Guanajuato, in the last five years the rate has tripled, so it's not limited to San Miguel. According to the federal stats, San Miguel (the *municipio*, which, with 160,000 people, is the equivalent of a county in the U.S.) had approximately thirteen homicides per 100,000 people per year."

Since San Miguel, the city, has a population of 75,000, the reader can prorate that estimate accordingly. I'm assuming most people thinking of coming to this part of México would live in or very near to town, but not always.

"Celaya is at fourteen or fifteen," Bossman went on. "We tend to think it's much more there than we have here, but that's not true. The cities and towns on the Michoacán border tend to go as high as twenty-four or twenty-five per 100,000. San Miguel is in the middle range."

Later, I checked the statistics for Chicago in the year of 2012, and the number of murders was eighteen per 100,000.

Detroit was fifty-three. Dolores Hidalgo, our neighbor to the north, has the slightly lower rate (than ours) of twelve. Let's give this more perspective and look at New York City, which used to be a very tough town just to walk around in after dark. How about Fresno or Biloxi, or even Minneapolis, my point of departure in 2007? Let's also look at Vancouver and Toronto. Minneapolis in this period came in with 10.4 murders per 100,000. Fresno was 10.1, and Biloxi was 2.2. New York City was an amazing 3.8, after peaking far above that in 1990. I don't have the number for how dangerous it used to be, but it was never anything close to 3.8. How about Washington, D.C.? It was 14, down from almost 18 the prior year. In St. Louis the rate was 35.5 murders per 100,000 of population. México City came in at 18, the same as Chicago, another big decline in crime for a city that used to be thought of as high risk. Los Angeles came in at a very reasonable 6.01.

Yet, in general, with 2010 numbers, the most current I could find, 4.8 Americans per 100,000 were murdered in the U.S. across all cities, towns and countryside, while 2.1 Americans per 100,000 were murdered in México in the same period. On the face of it, this comparison appears to be distorted, however, because most Americans in México were not here the entire year, thereby reducing the extent of their exposure to whatever risk they had in being here only a part of the year.

But a truer way to look at it is that the number of Americans supplying the base population expressed as per 100,000 is always changing as some leave and are replaced by others. But the total of per 100,000 is based on how many are here at any given moment. It doesn't matter if they are the same people from week to week, only the total matters. This same phenomenon takes place in the New York numbers, or in Biloxi, but the rate of turnover is much slower. These two numbers are generally trumpeted as proving México is safer overall than the U.S., which I do tend to believe on a subjective basis as well. While they are not very useful in analyzing a single place like San Miguel, they do undermine the American press contention that México is in general a more dangerous place than the U.S. I included them mainly because I see them brought up so often by México's defenders. Looking at these two numbers by themselves, as an American you are half as likely to be murdered in México overall as in the U.S. overall.

Not that the State Department displays anything but selectivity in these surveys. Even as they advise against travel to México because of the crime numbers, they have no problem with the Bahamas at 36 murders per 100,000, Belize at 42, or Jamaica at 52 murders per 100,000 people per year. New Orleans came in for 2012 at 53, close to the Jamaica number. On the other hand, it is not the job of the State Department to assess your risk at home, and if you don't ever see it spelled out in the headlines, you may think no risk exists. Much of this discussion is about what we are told, and who is telling it. My own sense is that something is being sold to us as well as told to us, and that is the problem.

Based on the numbers, Vancouver with 1.2 murders per 100,000 is the easy winner in this group. Biloxi, with 2.2 murders, was similar to Toronto with 2.0. If safety were the only consideration, the population in these places would boom with Americans headed north and to the Gulf, since the press has not warned them against Canada. At this point we at least can draw one conclusion: fewer Canadians are natural born killers.

But obviously this will not be the only issue in your decision. There are other chapters in this book to look at.

"Is there a political component to this?" I continued, winding down from a long series of calculations inside my head. Bossman was busy relighting his pipe.

"No," he said slowly. "Not for us. We've been careful to stay out of local politics, although we are aware that politicians will play to the voters in election years." For the current mayor, who cannot run again, that will be the end of his stint locally. The feeling here is that he may have loftier ambitions.

The city has recently added a mobile crime van focused on robbery, where the victim can make a report at the scene. A number of security cameras have been installed in troublesome areas, panic buttons set up in hotels, and the emergency operators are now bilingual.

"Does part of this problem also stem from poor selection and screening of household help?" I had offered no introduction to this tack, but based on my own experience and that of many expats I knew, it was a valid angle to examine.

He looked at me for a moment. "A good question. I think people, new homeowners and certainly tourists, come here with certain expectations of San Miguel. It's a paradise, they think, it's safe, or it's something out of Walt Disney. It's only after a few years that they realize that as much as we love this town, there are problems living in México, just as there are strengths. I think that people are often careless in the way they do some things. It falls under the heading of not being proactive, and the hiring of household help is probably in that category. People often don't ask for references (from a prospective employee). They don't get what we would call Social Security numbers, so I think that could be a problem. It's like walking around with a big pocketbook on the street at night and not taking taxis."

And I do see people unconsciously boosting their own risk. "Not to blame the victim," I said, "but might part of the solution be an educational program, a way of getting expats to recognize the risky behavior they engage in without realizing it? If you're out stumbling around drunk in the *jardín* at three in the morning, as I have seen more than once…"

"Yes, you're going to be a target."

"Right, so I'm not sure that as an expat or a tourist you can stand up and complain about crime in San Miguel. You may naïvely do things here that you would never do back in Topeka. Common sense applies, and if you don't practice any, then the risk factors creep out of the shadows and bite you."

"Absolutely. No question about it, even though, as you say, none of us wants to blame the victim. I think on the behalf of our organization, we've done a lot to educate, especially the expat community, in terms of the dos and don'ts in being proactive. As far as risky behavior, although you didn't ask the question, this three o'clock in the morning stuff, it happens as much to Mexican tourists as it does to expats and tourists from the north. I suspect that those who are targeted are often those young ladies out till two or three in the morning, drinking and standing in front of El Grito (a nightclub). San Miguel has become a playground for young middle class Mexicans."

"Part of my reason for talking to you is to give my reader a realistic comparison between routine crime here and in the United States or Canada, as for any town of this size. By routine I mean things not related to cartel activity. What's your sense of that? If someone asked you today, 'Am I generally safer in a Mexican town like this than I am in a typical American town of 75,000?' what would your response be?"

Another shrug. "Probably as safe if not safer. But then there's another part of the question. Is San Miguel itself safe? Yes, I think it's still relatively safe. But can it be more secure? Absolutely. That's what we're trying to do."

Bossman went on to explain that our neighbor to the north, Dolores Hidalgo, with a similar size and only 5% of the tourist volume we have, employs twice as many police. Our mayor has said there are no plans to add any in San Miguel this year. The police salary here is 4,200 pesos every two weeks, which at today's exchange rate is $328, or $8500 a year. This is not the kind of paycheck to encourage people to take greater risks in an already dangerous job.

"What is your personal feeling about the reporting of Mexican crime in the U.S. media?"

"I studied journalism, so I take that question very seriously. I think that on this subject, we are surrounded by lazy journalists. That's what the United States government and its corporate entities (partners) have done in terms of México as a whole. It's very unfair and the numbers are striking. Up until three or four years ago, of the entire U.S. tourist outflow, 4% went to México. It's now down to 2%. This is the only country in the industrialized world where those numbers are down. From every other country more and more people are still coming, that's why tourism here is still growing. A lot of publishers in the U.S. have been unfair with their budgets. They haven't allowed many of their journalists to come down here and make a full report. I haven't seen one U. S. article that gives a thorough representation of conditions here in central México. I think the best and fairest journalists come from the national media here."

"Can you ascribe a motive to this kind of distorted media treatment from the U.S.?"

"Yes, I can, and I think I can speak for a lot of Mexicans here too. Of course the American government is doing this. They want to keep the tourist dollars within the United States. That's their answer. By exaggerating what's going on here and not giving it a fair representation, they've hurt a lot of areas like our state of Guanajuato. Acapulco has had some problems, but what about Zihuatanejo, Playa del Carmen, or Puerto Vallarta or Huatulco (all beach communities), which are all still relatively safe?"

Thoughtfully, I brought this to an end. I said goodbye to David Bossman and walked up the hill to my own house. I was still troubled by the statistics, so as I walked I began to go over some recent murders in this town, not all of them in the past year, but the ones I knew about and ones that had made big headlines locally. In my detective fiction series I never use real cases.

In one situation, a woman was stabbed to death by her adopted teenage daughter. The girl had a long history of mental problems, and the neighbors testified to a series of screaming fights in the days leading up to the mother's death. The girl and her female friend were arrested for the murder. In another, a Mexican man who ran an organic food market was killed. The motive that I heard was a real estate dispute of long standing, but you can never be certain when the story comes to you second or third hand. The gossip mill cranks up to speed at any murder. Two older gay men died during a period of several years; each had a record of picking up young muscular Mexican men in bars. One was stuffed into his own refrigerator. A Canadian woman was stabbed to death in her home in a village about twenty kilometers from town. According to the only report I saw, nothing was taken but her life.

When we think about public safety in a town we're not completely familiar with, most of us typically imagine ourselves as the victim of a murder done by strangers, people we have not invited into our homes to clean or work in the garden, or for a one night stand, and who are not family members with either a grudge against us or an interest in our estate. It is also true that due to the sometimes selective nature of the local expat media, we don't always hear about murders among the Mexicans, but they contribute to the overall total numbers too, and they comprise the largest part of it, mainly because they are 85% of the San Miguel population.

I would like to think we can take this number of thirteen murders per 100,000 in San Miguel and parse it into categories based on relevance. How many of these situations really pose a personal threat to us? Isn't some part of that question governed by the risks inherent in our own behavior? I believe that by a measured lifestyle and being sensitive to risky situations we can reduce our overall exposure to something closer to that of New York or Los Angeles, if not that of Vancouver.

On a lesser scale, part of this issue is to avoid providing targets of opportunity. A common crime is someone lifting your wallet out of your purse that was left in the shopping cart while you studied the fine print on the label of a can of tuna. We need to bear in mind the vast differences in income between low-paid Mexicans and expats. The girl who checks out your purchases is making about $10.00 a day. The minimum wage of unskilled labor is around $5.00 a day. Your daily walking around money may easily be two or three weeks pay for many people. Another tempting target is your purse lying on the passenger seat of your car at a stop. Keep your car doors locked and the purse over your shoulder under your seat belt. There may be devices out there that can determine whether you have left a laptop computer or an iPad in your locked car—a debate still rages about this. These precautions are mostly common sense, but some vigilance is required.

Another issue is the common scam artist. There are some Mexicans who have brought this to a fine art. As a gringo, they see you as wearing an enormous target. Don't let people you don't know into your house, and anyone who knocks on your door with a line like, "Hi, I'm your neighbor, we met before," is bad news. Another common line is, "I need medicine for my sick little girl. It's 300 pesos." Sometimes they will show you a bogus prescription. The odds of this being in any way legitimate is as near zero as it is possible to get. A friend of mine was sitting in the *jardín* and was conned out of 1,000 pesos to pay for a tiny coffin for a man's dead baby. He said the funeral was that afternoon at the Parroquia. Feeling involved, my friend went to the funeral at the appointed time and found himself attending a wedding. Later that day, the same man approached him with the same story again, not even remembering his face. People wearing targets are anonymous; their principal feature is their vulnerability.

We would all like to be generous, and we are also aware that the money in our pockets represents much greater value to someone in real need than it does to us. Just remember the target. Donate to people you know personally that are in need, or donate through one of the many worthwhile organizations here. Being conned by cynical people does not enhance our natural feeling of being a good neighbor, and is only likely to make us less generous in the future on occasions when the need is legitimate.

Some awkward encounters may be inevitable. Yet, stout security on your windows and doors will send most burglars looking for easier access, and you won't be troubled by running into someone in your bedroom as you're going to bed. It's not as if they arrive towing a chest of burglar's tools on wheels. They bring what they can easily carry and conceal, just as you would. Ask who it is before you open your door. Many homes have intercoms. If you buy one without it, it's easy to install. The violent home invasions often occur when the burglar thinks no one is at home.

There is no perfect answer to safety issues, yet I think I come out on this question in about the same place as David Bossman, who has spent far more time on it than I have. "Probably as safe if not safer..." than a typical American town of a similar size.

If this answer is not perfect, you should not be surprised. The general numbers, while not that threatening, are slightly worse than I would have guessed, based on my own experience. If I had been searching for perfection, México would not have been my first choice anyway. It has other benefits that offset this defect, and I can't say what other place I would have gone to. But what I do know is that after my term in residence, I can live comfortably with what we have in the area of public safety, as in many other aspects of our lifestyle. It can obviously be made safer yet, and I'm sure San Miguelenses Unidos will have some impact as it develops.

In the meantime, I still sleep well at night, and I expect to sleep even better as time goes on.

CHAPTER 14

DOG LIFE

We can discuss the differences between our northern attitudes and those of México all day, but one of the best ways to understand some of them is to look at specific cultural mindsets, examples of how these norms express themselves on a day-to-day basis. A good place to start would be with dogs, because there is little common ground there.

As with most things in México, dog culture is stratified by class. If you are an upper class urban Mexican, you are likely to favor purebred male dogs. It would not be a stretch to think that you also regard yourself as ranking in the human counterpart to this class. The purebreds are likely to have come from Europe, as did your family. Having said that, because those dogs are not at risk, let's move on to the rest of us, who may not look at our roots in this way.

Branches of my own family, who fled Norway and Sweden in the nineteenth century, did not do so because they were possible rivals for the throne and therefore under threat due to their noble bloodlines. They were only simple people who had no visible future and thought they could do better across the sea, where class didn't matter so much and you could still acquire some affordable land. Upon arriving in Minnesota for that purpose, some were tempted to reconsider their choice.

Most Mexican dogs without AKC papers also fall into this same class, furry folks just trying to get by, or striving to improve themselves a bit from humble beginnings, although unlike the immigrants I mentioned above, the Mexican street dog is a native, going back in his heritage far more than the purebreds in México City, and particularly farther back than their owners. They are likely to have crossed the ice bridge at the Bering Strait with their Asian masters several tens of thousands of years back. It would take some DNA science to get into this, which is beyond the humble scope of this book.

You have probably driven around San Miguel and asked yourself, why are those dogs living on the streets as they are now? No matter which neighborhood you're thinking of living in, you may already be alarmed to see them everyday, mostly regarding you solemnly in groups, neither unfriendly nor welcoming. This indifference can be disturbing. On the surface of it, they don't appear to need us. Whatever happened to the idea of man's best friend? Sometimes they are sunning themselves on the cobblestones, just far enough off the main track to avoid being run over (usually). After you go back inside, they cheerfully poop on your tiny sidewalk, where it's unavoidable to your guests coming to dinner wearing white pumps. This is not what you lived with in Indianapolis, or ever expected when you came here.

Looking for some answers to questions like these, I stopped in at the S.P.A. facility at Los Pinos 7, a street that winds steeply up the hill from Calzada de la Estación, diagonally across from the bus station. The letters stand for Sociedad Protectora de Animales.

It was not my first visit to this refuge, because six years earlier we had adopted a street dog named Brownie. Her short hair coat has the color range of cinnamon, with dark eye makeup reminiscent of Cleopatra, and black leather lips; a typical look for a Mexican street dog. She weighs about sixteen kilos. When she joined us we fattened her up a bit with tortillas and butter. This convinced her of our good intentions even as it took her somewhat longer to understand our habits. For example, like many expats, we prefer to live indoors.

General Director Lynn Weisberg gave me a tour. Here the shelter houses up to fifty dogs and fifty cats. This morning it was at full capacity—its usual condition. Lynn Weisberg was wearing jeans and a work shirt. Being the chief executive of this organization is a hands-on job that involves more love than glory.

The dogs are housed in rows of cages, some singly, some in pairs according to temperament, over a rambling property. As we came in, many of them rose to protest that they were being held there in error, calling out to me, hadn't there been some mistake? Was I there to take them all home? Had I brought any treats with me? Others watched me calmly, while a few were literally bouncing off the walls, perhaps thinking I was recruiting for a circus featuring animal acrobats. The shelter can be a noisy place. As we passed the cage of one, she ambled over to the grill and looked at me hopefully. They all appeared to be well kept and cared for even if their level of adjustment varied. While the population of street dogs may be in some respects a community, it is not a fraternity.

"Amazing," said Lynn, her eyebrows lifting. "This one is scared to death of *everyone*. She always jumps back into her *tinaco* when someone new comes past. She must see something good in you." Suddenly I felt like St. Francis of Assisi, and I checked to see if any birds had landed on my hat. The *tinaco* Lynn referred to is a rooftop water tank with a wide mouth. Set on their sides, they make inexpensive and secure places within the cages for dogs to bed down in what might otherwise seem like a dormitory setting. It's their own space, where their back and flanks are covered. Think of your own dog hanging out under the dining room table for similar reasons. Mine has a worn beach towel. The security may be better there, but the instinct doesn't change much.

Up the slope are broad, graveled exercise runs, with a new set under construction.

I looked at Lynn for a moment. She's a trim, active woman whose engagement with the animals in her charge is clear and personal. She knows them all by name.

"These are the lucky ones, aren't they?" I said. "They might have ended up with the city."

"Yes, the Ecologia is responsible for the city dog pound, and that's the group that rounds up strays, or any animals that are wandering the streets off leash. They take them to the pound and the owners have five days to get up there and look for their dog. If the dogs are not found by their owners or adopted by then, they're euthanized."

The phrase, *on a short leash*, took on new meaning for me. Five days makes for a very short leash indeed.

"Of course, some don't have owners," I suggested, "even in the more approximate sense that you're using here. And your role is different from Ecologia."

"Our role is very different. We are a no-kill shelter, which means that when we accept an animal here we will not euthanize it unless it's very aggressive toward people or other animals, or it becomes so sick that it's not reasonable to try to treat it and then find someone to adopt it. This means that some of our animals that aren't adopted stay here for a long time, which ties up the cages. So we always have a waiting list for dogs wanting to get in, but I can't take them until I have a cage available."

"Who are the people bringing these animals in to you?"

"It varies. Many are animals people have found on the streets. Sometimes it's people surrendering their animals for various reasons. Maybe they're moving, or they're ill, or they found a dog and they already have as many as they can care for. We get them in a variety of ways."

Since the mission of S.P.A. is to care for homeless and unwanted animals and try to find permanent homes for them, it's not surprising that funding is always at the top of their list of concerns.

"So if I pick up a dog on the street and bring it in, I don't know whether it might belong to someone or not. Let's take a look at the dog culture here. I live in a diverse neighborhood in this town. Up the street a block from me is a high-end condo development occupied mainly on weekends by folks from México City and Querétaro. They drive cars far better than mine. Fifty feet away on the other side of me is a wedge of barrio that is very poor indeed. There are always dogs on the street and a fair amount of turnover. I know most of them by name. If I were just driving through as a stranger, what would I be looking at? How should I interpret this, because I think that most people traveling through San Miguel from the U.S. and Canada don't understand what they're seeing here in the street life."

"You're probably seeing some dogs that live on the street and don't have a home. They've either been abandoned and don't belong to anyone, or they were born on the street. Other times they are people's pets. It's common here for people to just open their doors and let their pets roam all day. The only way to really know is to see the dog often enough, and sometimes you know where they belong. They might also be dogs who've been surviving on the street for years and the neighbors feed them."

"So many are just marginally surviving, and you can recognize that."

"Yes, since many of the animals that are brought in clearly have been on the street for some time. Most of them are matted and dirty and in need of some recovery time."

"What is the charge to adopt here?"

"It's 350 pesos (at today's rate, $27.00 U.S.), which includes the vaccinations, the spaying or neutering, and we always include a package of food so they can transition from ours to their new food. We also operate a clinic here, not just for our own animals, but two days a week for the lower income people and for them we charge less."

I left feeling that S.P.A. is a colony, often a serious refuge for animals in desperate circumstances. It is not the absolute best place for them, not as good as a loving home, but it's far better than most of their other options, which are not diverse or plentiful, and the volunteers there do marvelous work.

Make no mistake, there are many people here in desperate circumstances too. México can be unavoidably raw in the way it presents itself. We all need help, and one way to cure ourselves is by giving something to others, because all expats possess more abundance than they realize. I just went online again to see if I could track down the source of a highly meaningful quote that I recall hearing long ago. Once again, I couldn't find the source, but it may have been D. H. Lawrence, who knew more than most of us about the subject: "México will break your heart," is the way it goes. People who push against this tendency give us all hope.

Another group that rescues dogs at risk of being euthanized is called Tres Señores, an equestrian ranch at the edge of town.

I was still reeling a bit from this encounter with canine San Miguel on the following day when I connected with Kelly and Jim Karger, who have an organization called SAMM, Save a Mexican Mutt. Kelly was the founder and it is truly her passion that drives it. We sat down in my own courtyard for a conversation. Sensing their good will, Brownie listened politely without interrupting, but took no notes.

"What is your view of the dog culture here?" I said. "It's clearly quite different from how it is in the U.S."

Kelly jumped right into this. "The attitudes about dogs here are completely different. We didn't realize that when we came here as visitors. I thought it was cool to see a pack of dogs running in the *jardín*. That was part of México, but after moving here we started to realize there's a huge difference. Those are either homeless dogs or they're dogs owned primarily by Mexicans. They don't do animals here like we do, especially dogs. They don't treat them like they're children. They are 'loosely' owned. Often they're the home alarm system."

"Do you think it's true that they're usually not house-trained?" From watching the dogs in my neighborhood, my sense was that they mostly lived outside. Many were certainly out all night. We experience what we call "doggie" nights, often those with a full or nearly full moon, and others that are quiet. Rainy nights are always quiet.

"Just naturally, if they're not puppies, they seem to understand. There is outside and inside, especially if they have been part of a Mexican household. We have very little trouble with those."

Jim added that in other larger cities, many Mexicans are adopting a more anthropomorphic view of animals and treating dogs closer to the way it's done in the U.S.

"What is the mission of SAMM?"

"Initially it was to rescue, rehabilitate, and adopt," said Kelly. "We started that when we moved here a little over twelve years ago. I've recently decided that we only have X number of dollars to put toward alleviating suffering. The best use of those funds is by spaying and neutering, and educating people on proper care and treatment. The majority of our funds and time are now focused on that. We go out into the campo at least twice a month, to the really poor areas and do proper sterilization."

"How did you get into this? Did you do it in the States?"

"No. We had three adopted dogs that we'd gotten from various rescues there. They came with us to México and we still have two of them. One is twenty and one is seventeen." She went on to tell how they rescued an injured poodle one night after they had been here three months. She's still with them. That's what started it all.

"She's a wonderful dog," Jim said, "and she's in great shape still."

"She's thirteen or fourteen years old now," said Kelly. "Then I got involved with the S.P.A. We started fostering litters of puppies, and of course there are only so many dogs that are going to get adopted at S.P.A."

"How did you arrive at your particular solution for the dog population problem here?" SAMM reaches across the borders into the U.S. and Canada to find homes for needy dogs.

"Well, we're a small community here, so we reach a saturation point very quickly. From my experience at the S.P.A., I figured we needed a bigger audience (of potential adoptive parents) so we joined Petfinder and started with that."

Petfinder is an Atlanta organization that showcases adoptable animals and adoption groups. "From there it became such a big business that I had to come up with a way to manage all these dogs and where they were going. Now I work with an organization called Rescuegroups.org. It offers services for rescue efforts like ours. They push out to about twenty other websites internationally, including Petfinder."

"What kind of preparation do these dogs typically need to go north?"

Kelly responded with a sober nod. "A lot. From the time we take one in—of course they usually have mange, they're emaciated, they have parasites—we get them straight to the vet. They get all their vetting done so they're healthy. Then we get them into a foster home either with us or another one. Their vetting has to be done by then because some of the foster homes have other dogs. We have to be sure they don't have something that's communicable. There's often a little quarantine period there. We photograph them and we watch their personality develop. Like, are they good with other dogs? How are they with kids, or cats? Then we offer them for adoption. We have a four-page application form. We try very hard to make a good match long distance with people, because once they're there…"

"Let me get this right. So these people are coming to you and filling out four pages of this form." I was starting to feel that this was patterned on human adoption agencies.

She nodded.

"And Kelly also has people all over the U.S. who'll do a home visit," Jim said. "That's another independent person who goes to that home and checks everything out."

"And we check their background references."

"This is *very* selective," I said. The Kargers were nothing less than canine social workers, and it made me think of how little respect Mexican street dogs get on their own turf.

"Yes," Jim added, "and she's adopted out more than 600 dogs."

Twelve years here, I was thinking. "You're averaging about one a week over that time."

"Right." Jim moved closer to the table. "We just got back from the States. We took eight dogs up to their permanent homes."

I had a different question ready, but really—"How do you travel with eight dogs?"

"When we had our van we had up to twenty dogs on one trip."

"And you keep them separated and amiable somehow? How does that work?"

"If they're large dogs," Jim said, "we make a little pallet for them and they just have to get along. Some of them are crated and then we're probably not the most popular people to show up at La Quinta when we stop for the night."

"Here they come again," I said. "By now they must know you even at the border. No one else is doing this."

"You would think so, and we've gotten to the point where we give them our business card every time, but they just don't remember. They all kind of smile and ask us, 'What is the purpose of your trip?' We tell them it's pet rescue, and we're bringing all these dogs up north..."

"How do you choose the dogs you're going to help?"

"Yeah, that's the tough part," said Kelly, shaking her head. This was a nearly insoluble part of the process. "I get inundated. I'll bet I have at least ten requests a day from people wanting help with dogs. Some are people who have a dog and want to relinquish it. We don't do a lot of those, unless it's a person who may be terminally ill. We have done that."

"How is this elaborate program funded?"

"We fund a good deal of it ourselves," Jim said. "Kelly also has some regular donors. There was a foundation that was contributing to it for a while, but then the board of directors changed and we lost that."

"Do you work with S.P.A. and Amigos Animales?"

"Not so much. We do sponsor a kennel at S.P.A., and I have worked with them in the past."

"Kelly sends a lot of dogs to Canada. We drive them to Dallas and fly them out. We just had our first European adoption, to the Netherlands." He went on to describe a Dutch concert violinist who fell in love with a Mexican mutt and had it flown in to meet her in Amsterdam.

"For people reading this book, how could they help you if they wished?"

"Our website is www.saveamexicanmutt.org."

When the Kargers left, I remained astonished at the extent of the effort they're making to rescue dogs from the rough and uncertain conditions of the street. Thinking of the cap on the population at S.P.A., Kelly and Jim Karger, in a given year, place for adoption a number equal to its entire dog capacity. It left me shaking my head.

San Miguel has a leash law. Like much other legislation, it can be difficult to say when and whether it's enforced. It may be that it requires a phone call to activate it. Knowing the consequences of being picked up and going unclaimed for five days, not many expats and very few Mexicans would make that call. I have seen recently a pack of about seven dogs working the Ancha de San Antonio area. If you're out walking your own dog on a leash, they could well be a hazard, or they may not. It's difficult to tell. When in doubt, there is a universal gesture employed here to keep dogs off: simply reach onto the pavement at your feet and bring up a stone, or just pretend to. It may not be entirely dependable, but I have never encountered a street dog that didn't know exactly what that meant, and at least pause reflectively before coming any closer. Most of them will run off. Of course, the majority of them are not a threat. They're usually just canine folks trying to get by as best they can.

Following my conversation with the Kargers, the

night remained warm, and I was still restless, thinking about the unexpectedly detailed reach of their program. After taking a long time to fall asleep, around two o'clock I was suddenly awakened by a commotion out in the street. With her low "big dog" growl, Brownie got up with me as I pulled on a light robe and went out onto our second floor terrace. The moon was nearly full as we both looked over the parapet, side by side. The intersection is also lit by two strong street lights. Brownie was puffing out her cheeks the way she does when she suspects there may be something dodgy afoot, something that needs to be looked into without delay, and with a forceful voice and attitude. She can effectively imitate the growl and bark of a dog three times her size. Below, in the cobblestone intersection off to the right, a kind of dress rehearsal was going on for what might have been a folk opera titled, *Who is the best Sentinel Tonight?* It was all singing and all dancing, with plenty of prancing about for macho effect. It's a traditional piece, and even though the name of the composer is long lost, the sentiment is timeless.

All the neighborhood dogs were there, treading their marks and taking their solos at center stage in turn. We know more or less where each one belongs. Here was Oso, a rough old bear of a dog with a red collar; his brown and black coat must have felt too warm for the season, but he wore it like a badge of honor. It was his costume that night as he laid down the dilemma of the story line in a broad baritone. Rash intruders, real or imagined, were threatening the security and peace of the barrio, the core of our *colonia*. They were strangers, foreigners, perhaps from a wicked place, so who was ready to answer the call to make this intersection safe for its inhabitants, both canine and human? Watching this made me realize that their concerns were not that much different from those of humans.

171

Next came Chispa, a full size character actor, a hero with half-length legs. Then the silver and white Lobo, the cocky leader of the pack with his spooky blue eyes. He was a romantic leading man at times, among the local sopranos, even when the curtain was down. Each had his own carefully worked out bit of choreography, his own scrap of melody, as the acting company faced an unseen audience down the slope of Cinco de Mayo. Some of their voices were commanding, others pleading, but each was eloquent in its own way. Then came Blackie, followed by two newcomers whose names I hadn't yet learned.

Silence followed, as if the invaders had taken their cue and chosen to pull back for an intermission. I waited, but I knew there were two others I wouldn't see that night. Poly, a true sentinel in his own right, was a possible tenor in this drama, wearing a well-used rough yellow coat that sheltered more than a few fleas, a working everyman character, but with elegant manners and a stout heart. He had for a long time accompanied his old friend Brownie on her morning walks, a fearless outrider who tolerated no nonsense as he kept the other dogs at a respectful distance. Relationships matter here, and not only among the humans, native or expat.

Finally, there was the one we knew only—and too briefly—as the Little Guy, a gutsy part Chihuahua mix that usually wore a royal blue knit short-sleeved shirt as he made his rounds in the morning. It had come from a human baby, but this guy was no baby. Sometimes I would see him six or seven long blocks from his home turf, strutting around with his inimitable style, but he was never lost, never worried. We didn't know his real name, we knew him only by his manner, which suggested he was ready for anything. I believe that was true. I hope it was.

Those two are gone now, as sometimes happens. I

hope they found a place for themselves that was a step up from our humble neighborhood, with our tiny, no-account venue for amateur theatricals, because they both deserved it. Perhaps they are at home in a warm part of Canada now, or maybe in Houston. I could even see that Little Guy in the Basque country of Spain. He'd look damn good in a beret. After all, why not?

I'll have to ask Kelly Karger if she had sent either of them on to a better place.

CHAPTER 15

THE JARDIN

San Miguel's Living Room

Any city that lacks a public square has always seemed soulless to me, and without a focal point. St. Paul, where I lived for many years, has two of them, which seems about right for a town of that size—300,000 or so. The square called Rice Park frames a vista for the surrounding public buildings, a way to get back on them a bit to better grasp the architecture and the very human scale. Part of St. Paul's appeal was always that it never got too big for its britches, as we used to say. With the addition of a sparkling new theater, it kept this collection of architectural relics as a matter of pride, an emblem of who it was and still is.

It also boasts a bronze statue of a native son, F. Scott Fitzgerald. He grips his hat in one hand, and carries a coat thrown over his arm, as if the day had turned out slightly warmer than he'd imagined. It's about life size, mounted at ground level, so you can walk up and say hello to him eye to eye. Perhaps mention what it was that moved you so much in *Tender is the Night*, or *The Great Gatsby*, as I have done myself more than once. Another local writer, Garrison Keillor, was the official patron of this project.

Like St. Paul, San Miguel also has two plazas in the

central part. One is called the Plaza Civica, where a statue of Christopher Columbus is displayed, but the principal people action is centered on the *jardín*, which I think of as San Miguel's living room. It faces the needle-like spires and façade of the Parroquia, not a cathedral, but officially a parish church.

This space, like any plaza should be, is a magnet for both visitors and locals. It is a place one block square that welcomes people of habit. If this town were in ancient Greece or Republican Rome, it is where we would go to vote. It would typically be surrounded by a market. Now, across the square from the Parroquia, we do have the old Presidencia, the city hall where the nation of México was born into a prolonged time of trouble in 1810. At one corner you'll see the birthplace of Ignacio Allende, the town's main, but not sole, revolutionary hero. This is an imposing two-story home built of grey stone, dominant in its position at the corner of the jardín. Now a museum, its tall ceilings easily accommodate people somewhat larger than life. The character of this house tells us that the War of Independence in México was imposed from above. It was not a grassroots affair, although as famine developed, it became everyone's cause. Over the entry, a sign in Latin gives notice that someone famous was born there.

On the other two blocks facing this plaza we'll find several sidewalk cafes, a bank or two, and some souvenir shops. On one parapet along the street, an assortment of newspapers is offered. On two other corners you can get your shoes shined.

The *jardín* boasts no statues, no monuments to famous men or women, although it is anchored by a bandstand in the center. For Christmas this focal point is turned into an elevated crèche, with the steps and approach on one side fenced in and devoted to live animals: usually a docile burro, a pair of good-natured sheep, and a chicken or two, that do not mind the annual attention.

In other seasons, Sunday afternoons—perhaps after the house tour—the *jardín* can be a good time to catch some *danzón*, the official dance of Cuba, and highly popular in México. Check Atención to see what's happening.

Most of this plaza is shaded by trees whose crowns are trimmed into smooth-sided drums. If you stand at the second or third level of any of the surrounding buildings you will see that their perfect forms are confined to the outside circumference only. Inside they remain gnarly and organic, highly individual, a forthright protest against the clipped formality of their façades. This illustrates one of the contrasts inherent in the Mexican character as well.

At eight o'clock one morning I walked down to the *jardín* to sample the action as it was getting launched. The May air was still fresh and cool. The thin haze we often have at dawn was burning off and I knew things would heat up by late morning. People, especially in retirement, parse reality in different ways, and a broad crew of expatriate men was already in place on the cast iron benches to sort out the most urgent issues of the coming day. Observing them, I could see their lives as a kind of serial adjustment, one that required a daily tweaking on the central ground to remain viable. You wouldn't want to wake up in a mode of serious catch-up; it was more about being alert and in harness when the first light hits your eyes.

I sat down next to two American fellows; one wore a fishing vest with many small pockets but no flies. The other was lighting what I thought might be his first cigarette of the day.

"I heard the rain's not coming at all this year," the vested one said. He offered no sources for this.

If that happened, it would of course be an agricultural and ecological disaster of unparalleled degree. I began to wonder if they had been talking to Al Gore online. I was searching for something more local in tone, so I got up and wandered on.

Just before ten I settled into the shadier of the two shoeshine stands. The proprietor was setting up. He had his client chair with two high footrests, his own humble stool, and two boxes of gear crisscrossed with frayed yellow nylon rope. From one of the boxes he took out four pair of women's shoes he must have collected earlier.

The shoeshine professional is a short, slender man with a dark, leathery complexion. His teeth have been severely mistreated by life. He wears a Coca Cola logo shirt and a closely woven straw hat with a single eye feather from a peacock's tail tucked into the band, lending a touch of upscale fashion to an otherwise patchy presentation. For fifteen pesos, a buck-twenty, he spent twenty-five minutes brushing and polishing my shoes to near-new condition. They are Eccos, a brand I order from the States, because I have to respect what my feet are called upon to do in this tricky walking town.

Meanwhile I occupied a seat worthy of a judge at Wimbledon, with a ficus tree as my umbrella, since the street I faced was five feet below the level of the *jardín*. From this lofty spot, as I watched, the city unfolded on its way to jobs, breakfast, dog walking, and school. Here and there shop girls washed and vigorously swept the stone-paved sidewalks fronting their stores before they put up their displays. Four cops in bulletproof vests, two of them women, chatted on the corner. The cool part of the day is also the calmer part of the day.

Above them, over the Rincon Don Tomás sidewalk restaurant, is the painting studio of Tom and Donna Dickson. Three people you have met in this book passed below my gaze without realizing they had made a second appearance, this time as a cameo, a walk on part with no lines to speak.

They were now local color. They made me realize once again how connected we all are here. Even as we chase our wildly different dreams, we all still share the same space without discomfort, the same condition of cheerful exile from the severe and judgmental northern country, where so few people understand how we could have done such a foolish and dangerous thing as to come down and live here in this lawless land.

I would only tell them this: that there is more than one kind of risk, and if the risk of being a crime victim is somewhat like it would be in the States in this size city, the risk of not fulfilling your *self* and your unvoiced ambitions up there is much greater than it is here.

And so I climbed down from my lofty perch and moved on. No one noticed me, which suited my task just fine. Even in the morning the shady benches in this common gathering place are taken first. As I walked away I decided to return at two o'clock, *comida* hour, as the Mexicans would say, to see how things had developed as the day heated up.

In that warmer afternoon I took up a position on the line of benches facing the Parroquia. This "parish" church boasts a tall neo-Gothic façade with numerous pink and spiny spires. From a modest distance, the texture of the stonework looks like a lacier version of something you might find in France. Closer, it is the detail that gives it away, because it is not the detail the French builders of Gothic cathedrals would have used. It has an improvisational quality that suggests the designer had never seen the real thing at first hand. It looks like a design he developed after studying photos, of which none were close ups. It may also be that the architect was interested mainly in the massing of the forms, and left the detail of their decoration to the builders' imagination.

Yet the feeling of it is still right for the *jardín*, where an accurate replica of a French cathedral façade would seem out of place. While it resembles nothing else in this colonial town, the Parroquia is still delightfully *local*, a unique piece of work that is the Mexican workaround version of the French ecclesiastical style. Now, this quaintly ostentatious parish church forms the background of every tourist's favorite photograph. As I sat there, four different shots were being lined up.

Aerial photos reveal another layer to this story, because the body of the church behind this Victor Hugo fantasy of the mid nineteenth century is of a different era entirely. It has the forthright form, and the thick and sturdy massing of the typical seventeenth century Mexican Catholic Church. It is a look that suggests the early builders knew about earthquakes and they weren't taking any chances. We are looking at a remodel here, essentially the graft of a new façade, an upgrade that would have been at once more upscale to a town of growing prosperity, but still reassuringly retro at the time it was built. Its message was one of growing sophistication—we may be a small city, it suggests, but we have captured a bit of the French culture here for ourselves.

This new façade is about twelve or thirteen meters deep, framing a porch and then a double entry inside. It is wider on both ends than the body of the church it fronts, which tends to mask the transition between the two for anyone looking at it from the *jardín*. This had to be the intention.

On the left end the new construction is connected to the façade of a school building, so the transition is masked. But standing at the outside corner near the right end of the front, the unresolved junction of the two eras and esthetic sensibilities is clear. On the exterior at the back edge, a blocky, much lower mass of masonry abruptly joins the graceful spires and continues back to the nave of the church at the distant end. The surface is much weathered, the connection confused. No real transition was ever attempted. It is as if the designer thought no one would be studying this mismatched union, and perhaps at the time it was built, another structure obscured this corner of the church from view. It has some of the sense of welding a newish Cadillac grill onto an old Ford pickup.

It may also be that the builders recognized that there was simply no plausible way to connect the two visually. The previous façade would have been plain and unassuming. The Parroquia replaced an even earlier church of the Sixteenth Century that must have been quite primitive. For the missing façade on the current church, there would probably have been a single bell, a tall entry, a pair of windows at the second floor, and virtually no adornment. At a certain point that's now hard to make out, it just wouldn't do anymore.

I wandered inside. The interior is roofed by a series of shallow domes, and the first one at the front ends smoothly at the rear of the second entry, as it had to. A partial dome will not stand. Here there is no jarring transition between the two eras. Nothing is visibly cobbled together, and the interior of the new façade is screened by the entry system, so the transition offers no startling change.

Within, the arches are all Romanesque, not pointed. The floors are ceramic tile that looks far too recent to be original. The normal glassed-in shrines and side altars line the walls. About halfway up on the right side is my favorite. Mounted on a column is a statue of St. Patrick, San Patricio, dressed in a bishop's ceremonial robes, with a vivid green cloak.

St. Patrick is not a popular figure in Mexican religious iconography. I know of no Celtic colony here, no bagpipe brigades marching in the local parades in tartan kilts. All I can think of for this connection is the Irish who volunteered to

fight for México against the U. S. in the war of 1846-8.
Outside in the *jardín*, the crowd has thickened. Many families with young children have arrived for the *comida* hour. More vendors line the paths and traffic-free streets, many now selling toys and balloons. The expat men's club has thinned, gathered up their newspapers, and mostly moved on. The black wrought iron benches in full sun are empty, the ones in the shade crowded. The afternoon heat has settled over the plaza, thickening in the trees.

I returned on an evening in the last weekend of July. It was the time of the annual GIFF, the Guanajuato International Film Festival. It divides its showings between here and the capital city. I found myself in Uptown Saturday Night. Turning the corner in front of the Eighteenth Century Canal family townhouse, now a bank, I encountered a twelve-foot *mojiganga* walking toward me. It was a puppet figure of a woman dressed in a black skirt and white blouse, considerably more restrained than they usually are. Just below the waistline I could see a narrow gash where the person inside could look out.

To me, *mojigangas* mean weddings, which is where you always see them, and as I approached the Parroquia, I saw the bride on the steps, waiting for a vehicle to pick up her and her party. The area between the Parroquia and the *jardín*, which I think of as the esplanade, was now filled with about 400 folding chairs and, at the far right end nearly against the Allende mansion, a covered bandstand. The Orquestra Valle de Santiago was just tuning up. This was a group I would have called a band, since they had no strings other than a Fender bass. It looked to be about thirty or so members. It had nothing to do with the wedding and everything to do with GIFF.

The band launched a series of swing tunes as two

matronly go-go dancers at the far end began their moves. I listened for a while and then moved through the jardín, which was not as crowded in the center as in the streets around the edges. On the bandstand several break dancers were working their moves to their own recorded music. On one side a clown in drag had attracted a large crowd on all four sides. The noise level was fairly fierce.

The surrounding streets were full of vendors of toys, souvenirs and food.

This was not the usual San Miguel crowd, which is mostly local with a large influx of expats and tourists from the north. That night, there were no more American and Canadian tourists than normal, but the contingent of Mexican nationals was larger, and both more varied and up-scale. This was a party that was going to run on well into the night, and I thought again about those expats who had bought houses in centro. As I left the *jardín*, the band broke into *Fly Me to the Moon*.

There is a webcam posted above the esplanade, so if you're sitting at home in the U.S. or Canada, and you want a taste of San Miguel's living room, you can catch some of the current action at any time of the day.

Simply enter this in your browser: https://www. google.com.mx/search?client=safari&rls=en&q=live-web-cam-san-miguel-de-allende&ie=UTF-8&oe=UTF-8&gfe_ rd=cr&ei=XrHXU5-kGaHI8gfA3YHQCA

CHAPTER 16

CREATIVE LIVES

In some ways, San Miguel owes its importance as an expat colony to a postwar migration from the States to study painting. The Instituto Allende, as it came to be known, was the old hacienda of the Canal family on what is now the Ancha de San Antonio. That, and the art school at the Bellas Artes, became dual magnets for Americans wanting to study in México on the GI Bill in the later 1940s and beyond. Word traveled north about an expatriate community building here, and others came down, writers like Jack Kerouac and Neal Cassidy somewhat later. Cassidy was found dead on the railroad tracks outside of San Miguel after a wedding celebration in 1968, although the cause of death was thought to be drug related rather than from an encounter with a train.

Writers and Writing

As a haven for writers the town continues to have some reputation today. Tony Cohan's popular book about San Miguel in the 1980s is called *On Mexican Time*. Although it appears to be out of print now, I still see a Kindle edition available on Amazon, and other sources are offering used and remainder copies on his page. The town hosts an active chapter of PEN International, the writers' organization. The San Miguel Literary Sala hosts monthly readings by local authors. A related entity, the San Miguel Writer's Conference, will soon celebrate its tenth annual session. There several well-known authors offer keynote addresses, and others provide breakout sessions and workshops on a wide range of writing topics. Regular attendance at the last conference ran just short of 300, although extra single tickets are sold for the keynote speeches and the audience can approach a thousand. Their blog is an excellent way to stay connected to their programs: http://sanmiguelwritersconferenceblog.org

In a broader sense, San Miguel is also home to many small informal groups and individuals who offer resources for editing, criticism, coaching, and the kind of mutual support that benefits a highly individual venture like writing. Over the years I've been a member of three different writer's work groups here, which in general have been highly useful. I know that others continue today. Although they're not always easy to find, if you attend one of the monthly Literary Sala readings, which are announced in the newspaper, in Atencíon's Que Pasa section, you can work the crowd and see what people will tell you about any groups they might know of. Or, you can join the Civil list and post a query there about this issue or anything else regarding life in San Miguel. Civil_SMA@yahoo.groups.com

The Library is also an ongoing venue for writers to bring their new works before the public through readings in the Quetzal Room. Not every group or activity will be right for every writer, so take the time to explore and ask questions before you commit. In these more intimate settings, personality matters, and your progress once enrolled will depend upon the blend of egos and approaches within that group. For the population size of this town, San Miguel offers an extraordinary concentration of writing activity.

For independent book production I prefer to use local

talent whenever possible. The cover designs of all my books have been done by the same graphic artist, Lander Rodriguez. My website was set up and is maintained locally by Julio Mendez. Interior design services for print books are available here too. The work of many local authors is sold at the Tienda in the Biblioteca (the Library) and at La Deriva in the Fabrica La Aurora.

The Tienda has been recently refurbished and boasts a lovely frescoed ceiling. The staff is friendly and well informed. Every book purchase supports the Library.

For myself, I had resumed writing for only the last two years I lived in Minnesota before coming to San Miguel, so it's difficult to make a comparison between here and Minneapolis as a hospitable community for writers. Certainly no one outside my family seemed to care much, but I hadn't produced a great deal of finished work by that time either, and I'd spent no time looking for groups to join. I would guess that there must be some. Writing is always a solitary occupation, no matter where you do it, but it is still somehow reassuring to know there are other wordsmiths laboring in the shadowy background all over San Miguel. I sit on my second floor terrace, where I have twenty-mile views over the reservoir into the mountains. I work outside every day, where back in Minnesota I could work at a cast iron table on my rear deck only about a hundred days a year.

I went looking for a perspective on this other than my own, realizing that no single writer represents this dedicated and independent group very well, so I asked Nathan Feuerberg to join me for lunch at Café Contento on Hernández Macias. It's a quiet place tucked away inside a building across from the Bellas Artes, where the Literary Sala readings are now held in the second floor auditorium. When I first met him six years ago in a writer's work group he had been expecting to move on in a few months. Nathan had lived and studied in several places in Europe by that time. Now he is associated with the San Miguel Writer's Conference in various capacities, one of which is managing their blog site, a venue where I have been known to furnish posts from time to time on the subject of the writing life in México.

Nathan is a slender guy in his late thirties with short-cropped hair and a low-key manner. He ordered a cappuccino and I asked for *chilaquiles*, a mass of tortillas mixed with shredded chicken, red sauce, and cheese. He talked while I ate.

"What is the writing scene like here?" I asked between bites, to get things started. "Does it draw a lot of wannabe writers, and can they find acceptance and support among the more established literati? I've heard it can be tough to break in here."

"There are a lot of people here writing a memoir. I don't know if I'd call them wannabe writers exactly, but they're writing more for family and friends. They're not as interested in publication; it's more like a time of life when they want to have something to show their family. Maybe they'll self-publish a limited run. You can also find a lot of artists here, writers who come down thinking they'll stay for about a year or two and work on their novel."

"By 'artists' you mean literary writers."

"Well, I guess I mean people who are serious about writing. People who have made a commitment to write. I meet quite a few people who are down here getting away from the U.S. or Canada to work on their writing."

"Is this a good place to do that?"

"I think it depends on the person. I was talking to Benjamin Sáenz a few weeks ago. He was here to speak at the Conference. He wrote *Everything Begins and Ends at the Kentucky*

Club. He was saying that he lives in Laredo, Texas, and he can see the border from his window. He was telling me that he can't really imagine himself coming down to San Miguel to work because he needs that violence there. He said he couldn't just be settling into this picturesque place. For some people, they're going to be better equipped to do their writing if they're in New York, where they're driven. For other people, like me, I need a tranquil environment. When I'm happy I do my best writing. For people who need a calm environment this is the best place for them."

Being a parent, I have written equally well in periods of chaos and of calm. I can do it either way because I'm driven wherever I am, but I greatly prefer calm as a background for writing.

"Does being a self-starter and being motivated go along with that?"

"Right. You have to be a self-starter here. If you're not waking up in the morning and doing your pages and spending your afternoons editing, you can quite easily be just hanging out and spending your time at cafes and gossiping with people, telling them you're a writer but not actually doing the work."

"Is there a lot of that going on?"

"I would assume there is quite a bit of it."

I knew there was, but I also knew that writing can be a matter of degree and application. I see a difference between being and doing. Being says, "I am a writer," but may not write much. Doing says, "I'm writing such and such a piece." It's an active condition.

"I'm working all the time," Nathan added, "but I've always worked all the time. Even on Christmas I write."

"What are you working on now?"

"Right now I'm working on a short story collection called *Exile Kingdom*, and all the stories are under 3,000 words, so the idea is that someone can read a story in one sitting. They're also all supposed to be ones that you could read aloud in ten minutes or so. They're more plot-driven than I've usually done before, but the plot still comes from relationships between the characters. I've also found these stories to be much more bare bones. They only include the essentials."

"So would you call yourself a minimalist, at least in terms of this collection?"

"For word choice and sentence structure I am. I try to choose every single word in a story, just like you would in a poem. Every verb in every sentence I try to make as exact as possible."

"Whose work do you admire among established authors?"

"I started writing because I was reading Henry Miller, the third book of the *Rosy Crucifixion (Nexus)*. I also like Angela Carter."

"What is it about Henry Miller? He was considered scandalous in his time because of his sexual frankness."

"He's really honest. That's what I always try to do with whatever I'm writing, to make it honest. People say that there is nonfiction, which is the 'truth,' and then fiction is supposed to not be the truth, and I've always thought it was the opposite. Good fiction has to be honest. Otherwise no one will believe it. Most of the fiction I write, even if it's using characters that don't exist, they're still based on my ideas, my values. I'm trying to be truthful about what I'm saying to people."

"In one of the workshops I gave at the Lake Chapala Writers Conference in February," I said, "I suggested that nonfiction doesn't exist and that the truth can only be found in fiction."

"I get into those arguments all the time."

"Does having an MFA in Creative Writing help more

with teaching others or with your own work?"

"I think having an MFA speeds up the process. The only way you're ever going to get good at writing is if you're writing every day, for a couple hours a day. But you can speed up that process. Let's say you write every day for five years, but if you do an MFA program, you're going to be as good as that in about half that time. In an MFA program, you learn a lot from your peers. Often, you can't see your own mistakes, but you can see the mistakes in your peers' work, and eventually you realize that you're making the same ones yourself. I was also writing a lot of surreal things before I did the MFA. Most of those programs follow the Iowa Writers' Workshop concept, which requires you to write realism. So I was forced for years to write realism, which I hated, but once I got good at doing that and then went back to writing the kind of surreal things I'd been working on before, I had the tools to make a surrealistic story work."

"So even in surrealism, the fundamental skills are still the best way of delivering your message." I enjoyed hearing this, because I am basically a craftsperson at heart.

"Right. You still have to ground your reader, and you have to use your basic tools, and those are the ones you're going to learn by doing realistic work."

"What is your purpose or goal as a writer?"

"If you disseminate your ideas, then eventually you'll reach a certain amount of people, and change their thinking, and they'll talk to other people. Your small idea may eventually have an effect on everybody."

"And who is your target reader?"

Nathan chuckled. "I think I have a niche market of about twenty-five people, all of them artists or writers. I always try to make my stories readable. You don't have to have a literature degree to get through them. A lot of MFA people don't get that. Your main objective is to communicate a message to another person, which is a lot harder than some people think."

"And at the same time, simpler. Do you see yourself down the road as mainly staying with short fiction, or can you imagine yourself writing a novel?"

"I primarily do short fiction, but I also have a novel I've been working on for years and I keep going back to it."

"What is the market like for short fiction now?"

"It's always been horrible, but it may be getting better. I have at least ten books on my nightstand that were written in the last couple of years, all short story collections, and I think it's because of the Internet. People don't have time to read long things anymore. They want something they can read on the subway going to work, or listen to on tape. I feel like this is the best time in the last twenty years to be writing short stories."

"Do you have enough time to work on your own projects?"

"I have in the last couple of months. I usually spend my mornings working on my own stuff. As we get closer to the next conference I'll have less and less time."

"Where do you see yourself in fifteen years?"

"Hopefully by then I'll have a novel. I'll be surprised if any of my short story collections ever gets picked up. With a novel you have much more of a chance."

Going off in search of my car, I left with the sense that Nathan Feuerberg had plenty of time. When I was his age I was locked in the middle of thirty-seven years of writer's block. I thought of it as silence. Without forgetting most of what I knew, I had still missed the creative middle entirely, although the home stretch seems to be going fairly well lately.

Painting and Art

Studying art or launching a painting career in a town as picturesque as San Miguel is a dream for many artists. The air is typically clean and sharp, people's faces are shadowed with character, and the toughest problem will be choosing among all the options for urban landscapes. The Instituto Allende still offers classes, as does the Bellas Artes. First, however, as a painter I would check out the numerous opportunities to learn from working artists in their studios. As they ask you what you're doing, you can also ask them what *they're* doing. You can see it on their easel. This is the centuries-old traditional method of studying art, and it's unparalleled for hands-on attention and a personal connection. One such studio I am familiar with is Donna Dickson's at Galeria Dickson, #1 San Francisco, second floor, at the corner of the *jardín*. She shares this gallery/studio with her husband Tom, who supplied the painting I used on the cover of my first expat book, *San Miguel de Allende: A Place in the Heart*. The fabulous scene on the cover of this book, Day's End, is his too. There are a number of other artists who also give lessons. For a finely finessed watercolor style, Kelley Vandiver teaches small groups or individuals in his studio in the Fabrica La Aurora.

Although you will find art galleries all over this town, the greatest concentration of them is in the Fabrica La Aurora. It is located on Calzada de la Aurora in the northwest corner of the city. A former fabric and shirt factory, it is now full of studios, galleries, antique shops and a restaurant and a coffee shop. It usually hosts an art walk on the first Friday of each month. Interestingly, in making the transition from a decades-old factory to a lively art center, the property did not change hands—the sign of a nimble and creative ownership.

One of the most prominent galleries in the Fabrica is owned by William Martin. I stopped by one morning to have a chat with him and his wife, Raé Miller, also a painter whose gallery of her own encaustic paintings is just around one corner. They are also both active in giving painting lessons. Raé's work is abstract and subtly colorful with the soft and subtle changes of mood that, for her, only the encaustic medium can provide. With their sense of movement, these paintings tend to subtly track her life story through their curves, layers, and textures. The intimacy in her painting easily draws the eye and holds it. It is a journey through life.

Bill Martin's work is straight up traditional and representational, clearly drawing on the examples of past masters. He brewed us each a cappuccino as we sat down to have a conversation in his working studio behind the gallery space.

Raé had told me that she had already read some of my mysteries, so she knew that my detective character, Paul Zacher, had begun (and continues to be through all the cases) as a working painter. That's his *hook*; it helps him to see things differently, as any painter must do.

"Can you each tell me something about your background in art?" I began. The path into an art career can be a tortured one. Bill started. His hair is white and he wears a goatee that reminds me of van Dyke.

"I've always drawn and painted, not with oils but watercolors, since I was a little kid." As if holding a brush, his hands moved graphically as he spoke. "I studied architecture in college, until I realized that wasn't my thing. I was only taking it because it seemed close to art. I got a part time job with an architect one summer and I decided to change my major to art. I had just read *Lust for Life*, the story of Van Gogh. I was inspired by it."

I thought of the 1956 movie, with Kirk Douglas as Van Gogh, and Anthony Quinn, who could bring an essentially crude vigor to any role, as Paul Gauguin. What was it about? In a word, passion, the first tool in the artist's paint box. It has a role in every brushstroke, every line.

"Irving Stone's book," I said. Stone had caught the tone. "I took about a month of that art major. The classes were really crazy, all abstract, and I wanted to learn classical styles first, so I quit college. I felt like I'd been going to kindergarten every day, cutting up papers. Then I found an artist who had just moved from the Virgin Islands, and I started taking lessons from him. I became his assistant. I took over and taught for fifteen years while I studied. I started my own school and continued to teach while I started my own gallery."

"Where was this?"

"California. I showed in Beverly Hills, then in Carmel."

Then came a deal in Aspen, Colorado. Martin began showing there and in Santa Fe, but a change in the art world set in after 9/11, as it did in so many other areas. When the art market cooled he started to look for a different scene.

"I thought about San Miguel then because I was born in México City. We moved to Los Angeles when I was three, and I grew up spending summers in Querétaro with my grandparents. I'm half American and half Mexican."

Through a series of visits over the years, he had always maintained his family contacts in México.

"I always remembered that and I started thinking about coming back and opening a gallery. I also thought of Cuernavaca, but I heard it had changed. My sister said to me, 'Why don't you check out San Miguel?' I had come here in 1968-69, and it was a dusty little town overrun with hippies."

"How about you, Raé?" She's a youthful-looking blonde who appears to have hit her stride at a pace that's not going to wear her out, since it gives something back for all the effort that she puts in.

"My mother was a painter as a hobby. One day I came

home, at twelve or thirteen years old, and she was just finishing up after painting. There were still paints on her palette. I said, 'That looks like fun, can I try it?' and she handed me a small canvas board, some brushes and a palette knife, and she said you can use whatever is left on the palette. I never picked up the brushes. I created a painting that was very textured. I was lost in it for a couple of hours as I fell in love with painting. Unbeknownst to me she entered it in a contest. It won first place locally, and second in the state.

"We were moving all the time then, and we had just arrived in Alamogordo, New Mexico from Thousand Oaks, California. I was feeling very displaced. Painting gave me a way to connect. At that point I started taking every art class that I could find, so I kept my hand in. I wasn't offered the option of college, so I went to work at an early age, I think I was about sixteen when I got my first job. I went straight to work from high school. I still had the art as a background, but I was never able to focus on it. It was really my way to communicate, because I was always the new kid, always moving."

"Were you from a military family?" I had picked this up from the Alamogordo connection. Raé looked at me for a moment, and I felt the conversation had subtly changed direction.

"My dad was a civilian contractor for the military. We moved every couple of years to wherever the bases were. I've lived in more than thirty-five cities. It became a habit for us to move. After I left my parents' house I kept doing it on my own."

At that point I began to feel there was a greater significance in her choice to settle here in San Miguel, as if it was a way of coming to earth after a long and rambling journey, where the destination, always determined by others in the earlier years, was never very clear.

"My father died suddenly during the Cold War while

he was on a business trip to Europe," she continued, with no special change in tone. "A very young man, he was forty years old. They didn't notify us for ten days."

For ten days. Hearing this the detective writer in me wanted to turn this story down a different path, but my inner editor reined that thought in.

"We were dealing with his top secret clearance and other things I didn't really understand. I was devastated, and the art was always a direction I could do for myself, more for my own wellbeing than anything else. It's an internal thing for me, not just about being part of the art world. I've been lucky because I've had work that was well received. I've had a professional studio since 1998, even though I was still working in real estate. I've had several incarnations, but real estate was the most successful one, and a good fit. As I moved here I saw the property market was ready to do a nosedive, and I decided to step out of the business and take a leap into full time art. I had visited here in 2004, and saw an opportunity, because I had owned a gallery in California, but I couldn't afford to keep it. It was so expensive there. My art progressed from oils and acrylic to watercolors, and finally to finding encaustic. And that's where it really flowered."

"Whose work do you most admire and why?" Bill took this question.

"There are so many artists that I like, but I have to say those of the Victorian period, and especially the pre-Raphaelites. Not all of them, but I really like John William Waterhouse. I also love the Impressionists and John Singer Sargent, Joaqín Sorolla."

"Even going back to the Academic painters," I said, "they were masters of technique, even if some of their paintings were brainless at times, they certainly had the process of painting down." I was thinking of Adolphe Bouguereau, an

extremely successful academic painter whom the Impressionists detested, yet whose mastery of technique, color design,
and command of light had then and still has few peers. It's
his sentimentality that always makes people wonder today
what he was thinking. We can never ask artists to think like a
contemporary of ours, but when they are prone to the weakest
cultural features of their own period, their reputation inevita-
bly declines over time.

"In anything," Bill went on, "the furniture, the architecture. To me it was a really interesting era."

"I really admire the work of Helen Frankenthal-
er," Raé said. "Then, Monet, Renoir, Odilon Redon and
Cezanne. I've always been moved by the Impressionists."

"What makes this town a good place to be a painter?"

"It's kind of a simple place," said Bill. "It's like going
back in time. We can walk to work and it all has a creative
vibe. Since I've been here, there's the writing, the music, painting in different styles, there's something about all of it that
you can't really define. First of all, it's just so picturesque. For
thirty years I went to the beaches. And then I came here, and
it's like, wow, it's a magical little place."

"It's easier to be focused on art here," Raé said, "and
it's less materialistic. Even if you aren't making the quantity
of dollars you would need in the United States, the quality of
life is really good in San Miguel. We were talking about that,
because sometimes we get a little frustrated, and we think, I'm
tired of living in a third world country, and then Bill reminds
me that we have a lot to be happy about. I have more time to
devote to my art here because of the pace and because it's affordable. Even though it's getting more expensive than it was
when I first saw the place, it's still more affordable for artists
here than in other places. There is also good art patronage
here. It has changed, and it was previously more American

and Canadian, but now we're getting more people from México City, Querétaro, Guadalajara, Monterrey, San Luis Potosí. They're all coming here on vacations and they're buying art." Bill went on to describe their clients as more sophisticated than in some other places he's worked. They already know the work of Sorolla and Sargent, and they're able to talk intelligently about what they like.

I asked Bill and Raé what inspired them.

"Life, beauty," he said. "It's hard to put into words, because I can just look at something and I feel like painting it. Usually it's because I feel it's beautiful or there's something that needs to be said about it."

"When I was painting I sometimes wondered whether you really needed to start with beauty. Can't beauty be something you develop in the process of working on a picture?" My own painting has been overwhelmed by writing since I moved to México.

Bill felt it has to be something you add, because the picture has to come out beautiful, not just pretty.

"I get inspired by revelation as I'm working," added Raé. "I also have ideas about what I want to do, but I like it unfolding in front of me. There's an intuitive quality to it, and I enjoy scraping back in and making layer upon layer. I do a lot of series about water, with that whole mystery that comes out in layers as you look further in. You see things that are veiled. I have issues with memory, and that inspires me, how I can't quite remember things the way they actually happened, or sometimes in which year or location. There's a visual aspect that goes with a memory, and I want to capture that—I don't often paint real things. It's more intuitive."

Bill does portrait work, and unlike some painters, he doesn't consider it a lesser discipline.

"Actually painting the human face or figure is the ultimate for me. You're not trying to capture the surface, to only make it look like the person, you're trying to get the soul. It's like a landscape. You're not just painting trees, you're trying to paint the essence of the landscape. There are all these things I could never write down, so I paint them."

Both Raé and Bill teach their style of painting. The kind of student they get varies with the season, and many are local residents. I was surprised when Bill said that many of his students only paint when they're present to take a class. They go back up north and drop it for the rest of the year. I always thought that painting involved more passion that that.

"What would you do if you weren't a painter?"

"I'd be a writer," said Raé.

"I'd be a musician," said Bill. "I'm learning the guitar and I play harmonica. I'd also like to be a fisherman."

"Part of me misses the organizational side, the business side of things," added Raé. "I have a business brain and an artistic brain."

"Artists literally see things differently. What does that mean for you?"

"Well," said Raé, "I find myself being an observer. Sometimes I may be sitting here but I'm really up here (in my mind), watching, looking at the whole picture. In seeing things differently, I think we take in different details. My life here is a lot like that, instead of just passing through. There's a lot of richness here to discover. When you go down to the *jardín* and watch people going by, there are different levels of doing that. Sometimes you're seeing blocks of color, and other times the details that make life here what it is. There's a certain sweet bite to it, the interaction of families, and how much time they spend with their children. You see them carrying their kids all the time. In looking at it differently, I see the relationship of people as an observer."

"I think artists see the essence of things," added Bill. "They get right down into the heart of the matter. That's what I might want to paint, when someone else might see something completely different. I can see a tree, and what I think is the essence of the tree, another artist might see abstract shapes or colors. I think we get down into the heart of things like musicians do. Artists see things truer."

"I think our brains work differently," she added.

"Is this the life you always imagined yourself leading?" Both laughed.

Bill shook his head slowly. "Not really. I try not to think about it. You don't know what's going to happen in the next five minutes. I try to enjoy the ride. I think I'm pleasantly surprised because I'm doing things I never thought I'd be able to do. I like who I'm becoming as a person. I have important things to say. That's critical to me. I enjoy what I'm doing. I'm happy."

"I wanted to be able to paint all the time," said Raé, "to sell my work and be a successful artist, to have my own studio here, to relate as a teacher and to have some success in the U.S. as well. I also really wanted a good relationship with William, and here we are, married two years ago. I think you can direct your own life. A lot of people don't ever bother to sit down and do that. They make other kinds of plans, like financial plans, but what about the heart of it?"

"Indeed."

Acting and Theater

A number of years ago I was traveling north through Greece by car, after crossing the Adriatic and landing by ferry at Patras from Brindisi in Italy, and I stopped overnight in the modern town of Delphi, which is situated on a bluff directly above the ancient city. I planned to tour the ruins in the cool of the following morning, since this was in the middle of July.

In those days the modern population was about 15,000, and it was easy to walk out into the country, which I did that evening toward dusk. I had gone less than a kilometer when I observed a man emerging from a gate in the fence that edged the slope overlooking the old city. He quickly moved past me and I waited for him to get closer to town before I slipped through the gate he'd exited. I'm not sure what I expected to see, but it felt like a subtle invitation.

Descending through a scattered olive grove for fifty meters or so, I gradually entered a steeper terrain. Below me the ancient city spread out on its ledge, and across the valley loomed Mount Parnassus. About a hundred meters down was the upper rim of the Theater of Apollo, beautifully preserved, if not fully intact. And down at the stage a play was in progress, a dress rehearsal, because there was not a single other person present in the seats. I took a place eight or ten rows down and settled in, feeling like an intruder, hoping to be nearly invisible in the failing light. As far as I could see, no one else was in view anywhere else in the city.

I speak no Greek, but the tone and costumes below told me I was watching a classic drama contemporary with the theater itself. It would have dealt with archetypal relationships and their violation, or with the triumph and subsequent failure of a flawed character. The music was unearthly as the shadows settled among the ancient buildings surrounding the theater—the Oracle of Delphi, that within the sacred precincts of its cave held the *omphalos*, the navel of the world, and was a world pilgrimage site then; the Treasury; and the Temple of Apollo. The lights came up—it would have been torchlight for the performances in those times—and I was whisked without protest to the world of four or five hundred years before the start of the current era. Even without knowing the play or its message, I was deeply moved, as if I had been transported back in time.

An hour later, in the starlit darkness, I climbed back up the slope and found my way through the gate. I couldn't help but think as I walked back to the modern town, how theater is one of the most ancient of the literary arts. Certainly painting and sculpture are much older, but for those works that require speech, drama and poetry must be the oldest. When this 5,000-seat amphitheater was built about 2,400 years ago, the tradition of the theater was already in an advanced state of development, and was properly thought of as high art. This huge and sophisticated building would be playing host to a familiar and long-established repertoire, much of which has been lost. Yet this same medium lives and prospers all over the world today, even in our small mountain city of San Miguel de Allende. I could only think that is because it must still be highly relevant. Something about it continues to move us as it always has.

I was again going over this experience and the idea of theater as a cultural mainstay of both Eastern and Western civilization as I sat down with Jim Newell, who is deeply involved in the theater scene here in San Miguel. He has a Ph.D. in Theater Arts from Wayne State and has been active in theatrical productions both as an actor and a director for nearly forty years. I began with a question of theory, which I wouldn't have asked if I hadn't known he had started with an academic background where he may have encountered this idea before. I had told him earlier about my evening in Delphi so long ago.

Newell is in his sixties, average height, with a trim and active build. His engagement with the subject suggests retirement is not in the cards for him.

"Jim, let's start with the larger picture here. What is

the role of theater in our society today? Why is it so lasting, and why is it still relevant in these times? Why are we even talking about it now? I can think of few things in our culture with that kind of staying power."

"Going back to your evening at the Greek theater—theater started as a means of entertaining and also educating. It was a communal experience. The word tragedy actually comes from the Greek word, *tragos*, which means goat. They used to sacrifice a goat before the plays."

I had never known this. Certainly that part of the ancient tradition had been lost when I used to go to the Guthrie Theater in Minneapolis.

"Originally it was choral, and one part of the chorus would make a comment about whatever the situation was and the other one would respond. Out of that came the first actor, he was named Thespis. He stepped forward from the chorus and became a singer and a character. That's where we get the name Thespian.

"The Greek tragedies were for the most part based on larger than life characters: kings, princes, nobleman, great warriors. It was to show their hubris, in other words, they reached beyond themselves and in that sense they destroyed themselves."

"What was the message in that?" I was thinking that this sounded a little like *keep your head down*, essentially a leveling effect, yet many Greeks were known as original and pioneering thinkers in architecture, sculpture, philosophy, and mathematics, which is why their culture is still so influential today. Our public buildings in Washington mimic their style to evoke the legitimacy of democratic government.

"The educational intent was to elicit the emotions of pity and fear. It was the catharsis of pity and fear, the cleansing of it, that is the point that the playwright is making. He wants us to empathize with the character, and to fear for him. And at the end, pity him, because he has ruined himself.

"The comedies were meant to entertain, obviously, but also to show the foibles of everyday man, his futility and humorous situations, and overextending himself in a comical way. Those are the two sides of it; you always have the masks of comedy and tragedy. Why has this continued? Because, as Shakespeare says, theater holds up the mirror to nature and shows us ourselves. Once again, it tells a story in which we can empathize with the characters, and feel pity and fear for their situations. That has continued through the ages. That message is not as apparent today as it was in Greek tragedy."

"And the theater provides a place for the community to come together."

"Exactly. To be in an audience, no matter what the size, is a shared experience. There's nothing to replace it."

"I can see that."

"You can sit in a darkened room and watch television by yourself, but you won't get the same experience that you would in a larger room with other people. Because it's all about the synergy between the presentation and the audience that creates this immediacy and appreciation of the play. As an actor you can feel and sense it. You can sense when you're connecting with an audience and you can sense when you're not."

"Are you reading their body language or facial expression when you're performing?"

"No, because you don't want to look at the audience per se, it's not that direct, although you do sneak a look at them now and then. The energy that's emanating from them is palpable, and you can feel it."

This is undoubtedly what draws established film actors to work in live theater at far lower pay than they can earn before the camera. It's the instant reaction of the attentive audience, the responsiveness that is never available on the fifth or the eighth take of a two-line close up with a reaction shot. The excitement is of a kind and degree that the film set process cannot provide.

"Theater," Newell continued, "appeals to the imagination. In the Greek theater the actors wore elevated shoes and used masks to create a larger than life appearance. We think that inside those masks were something like small megaphones. There were no real sets. Everything about the location was told to the audience: we are here, we are there.

"The magic is in its appeal to the imagination. As Coleridge called it, 'the willing suspension of disbelief.' In other words, you willingly walk into a theater, sit in front of a stage and believe that whatever is being presented to you is real. That's the audience's commitment in the shared experience."

"Is there some magic in seeing actors perform the lines we could simply read ourselves? Some people do just sit down and read a play."

"You could, and then it becomes a poetry reading. It doesn't embody the full aspect of the theater: sound, gesture, speech, music, and spectacle. You don't experience the movement."

"And it's the entire range of nuance," I added, "that any actor brings to the role, which is composed of his or her process that is not explicit on the page, although it may be implicit."

"Exactly, reading between the lines. That's the actor's craft. To sit and read it you may get some sense of it, but not the full impact."

"As an actor, what of your own experience and character do you contribute to a role? Suppose it's a Shakespeare history play. Certainly we all have an element of Falstaff in us on a Friday night after getting off work, but what does your life experience bring to the role of Henry V or Ophelia? And if that works, can you also then go on to do Willy Loman (*Death of a Salesman*) just as well?"

"Yes, of course. The purpose of the actor is to portray the emotional life of the character as honestly as possible. If you have life experiences that correspond to the same path that this character is taking, all the better. But they're still all human emotions. You say to yourself, what if? What if I *were* this person, faced with these problems, what would I do? You bring your human emotions and experience to that situation. It doesn't matter whether it's Hamlet or Willy Loman, they're still human. Hamlet is a little more elevated person, where Willy is more the common man. It's still in either case living the emotional life of the character as honestly as possible."

"Can you describe the theater scene here as you found it when you came to San Miguel eight years ago?"

"I knew nothing about it, to be perfectly honest."

"Are you saying that it wasn't part of your decision to move here?"

"Right. When people say, 'What brought you to San Miguel?' I say, 'My wife.' But I found myself in the lobby of the Santa Ana Theater one time, and this gentleman was talking about producing *A Man for All Seasons*. I walked up to him and I said, 'Oh, that's interesting. I'm an actor. I've both appeared in the play, and I've directed it. I'd like to be a part of it.'

"He said, 'Well, I'm going to have a reading. Why don't you come and participate?'

"So I came, and I gave him a picture and a résumé, as I would in any professional situation, and he said, 'What are you trying to do, impress me?'

"I said, 'Yes!' Then he was trying to give it back to me, and I told him to keep it because I had a thousand of them. So, the outcome of that was that I ended up playing Sir Thomas More. It was good experience and a good production. We sold out and had people sitting on the stairs. That was my first experience with the theater scene in San Miguel. At that time there were two different groups operating out of the same space, that Santa Ana Theater in the Biblioteca."

"How has it improved since then?"

"There are four or five producing units here now. It's been more cooperative because we're all using the same talent pool. That pool has grown, and we're getting more young people now."

"You don't have to use sixty-year-old ingénues anymore."

He suppressed a smile. "Exactly. That's been a big progression."

"What is the Shelter Theater? Isn't that a third option? It's not too far from where you're going to be located with your new venture."

"It's a small space, only about fifty-five or sixty-five seats. So it's limited to more static performances."

"Is the theater audience here big enough to support all these efforts? Although, the way you describe it, it's not like the productions are simultaneous. Because they're using the same space, they have to be sequential."

"There are 8,000 expatriates in this town at any one time. Five thousand are here permanently."

"Sure." My numbers are even somewhat larger than this, but the sources are mainly guesswork at best.

"The focus of my new theater project is toward them, since I'd like to be selling the subscription series. One of the problems with the theater scene here is that there are only two venues now. There's the Angela Peralta, which is really a theater, since it has flies and everything."

The Peralta is a classic and intimate Victorian era theater that's been carefully restored. It plays host to every kind of performance, even opera. It's named for Angela Peralta, Mexico's leading opera star, who died of yellow fever at the age of thirty-eight in 1883.

"You would probably prefer to work there."

"But it's always overbooked. You don't have time to rehearse in there. All you have time for is two or three days to come in with your production, set it up, and run it for a weekend or four days. The Santa Ana, which is a nice little theater, is also overbooked and overused."

"How big a space is that?"

"It's eighty-two seats, so it's a little more than the Shelter Theater. My new theater will have a three-quarter thrust stage with seating for about 125. The reason I'm doing this is because of the overbooking of the other spaces. Plus, at the Santa Ana you run into the same problem. You can only rehearse in there one week before you open, from ten to one o'clock. Then they have a movie in there or something like that. The weekend before you open, the theater is closed because the Library is closed. (The Santa Ana is in the same building as the Library.) Your last regular rehearsal is on a Friday, then you come in on Monday and you have a tech rehearsal, then you have a dress rehearsal on Tuesday, and you open on Wednesday. There was a big meeting about the use of the Santa Ana. We tossed around a lot of ideas, but the bottom line was that you just couldn't use it sufficiently as a rehearsal space prior to production, and it's so important to be rehearsing in the same space in which you're going to perform."

Newell came up with the idea of leasing a *salon de fiesta* that had been used in several theater productions a few years earlier. It's on Independencia, not far from the belt road, (the *libramiento)* and it has its own parking.

"The owners were willing to give us exclusive use of the building for a year with an option to extend. One of the things about the Santa Ana is that for the most part it's not reserved seating. So prior to the doors opening you've got the crowd wedged into the small space outside waiting to be the first to get in. It's often hot and there's only one exit."

In the new theater no seat will be more than twenty feet from the stage, which will be elevated.

"Is there a risk that this will be too many hats for you to wear? Do you enjoy being the businessman in this venture after spending so much of your career on the creative side?"

"Well, I've been around theater long enough that I know the workings of it. I'll be the managing director, as well as the artistic director initially. I'm not going to perform, except possibly in one show a year. I'll have other directors too. In order to fill the space, between major productions, of which there will be four, I'll have one-person shows, standup comedians, and I'll have small music concerts. Once again, they would have adequate rehearsal space and time. That's my dream."

"As the artistic director, what drives your selection of plays?"

"The first season, having been in repertory for four years at Wayne State, I saw the pattern of their selection. It's a comedy, a drama, a classic play, meaning Shakespeare or an American classic. Then a show to be announced, either a small musical, or a new play. Initially my attempt is to appeal to the audience with not necessarily a show they know, but one they'll be comfortable with, knowing what it's about."

"How do you obtain the rights to produce a play?"

"Now, that's an interesting question. You write to whoever holds the rights to that play and obtain permission for a fee, a royalty fee, that is based on the size of your house and the price you charge per ticket."

"Some plays must be in the public domain. The copyright limitations apply there too."

"Definitely. That's why you want to do some plays from among that group so that you're not spending a lot of money on royalties. That's the idea behind having the classic presentation."

"What should we expect from the new San Miguel Theater Company?"

"I'm in the process of turning this new venue into a comfortable, accessible, enjoyable theatrical experience."

ॐॐॐॐ

For current theater events use this link to Atencíon, San Miguel's bilingual newspaper: http://www.atencionsanmiguel.org/category/arts/theater/

Another valuable resource on cultural opportunities of this kind is the San Miguel Civil list, one of the Yahoo groups. You can join and receive their regular postings by email. As a member, you can also ask questions, but it is good to do some Internet research first before posting a query. Anyone thinking about relocating to San Miguel will find this an excellent way to keep up with current activities, although you may find you want to be selective about much of the material posted. There are currently about 8500 members. Here's the URL: https://groups.yahoo.com/neo/groups/Civil_SMA/info

CHAPTER 17

AN OLD MEXICO HAND

I imagined at this point having a conversation with someone who had been down here for years, not merely seven years like me, but twenty or more, a person who remembered the times when you couldn't find a shower curtain or good ground coffee, when if you were planning a dinner party, you went to the store before you invited anyone, just to see what you could buy that day. A person who had seen some serious changes, had seen the different kinds of gringos come and go, both as travelers and expats, had seen the culture change *poco a poco*, but not that much, to accommodate this invasion from the north. And beyond the culture, he would've seen the city grow, the infrastructure develop, and technology advance to the stage where a person could work online from his second floor terrace, as I am at this moment.

That's how I found Jim Priest. He's the kind of guy you would have seen around town for years, even back then. He's nearing his mid sixties now, has a white ponytail, and is always on foot and wearing shorts. He's got a tall frame and an active build. I've often seen him around town myself, and I finally learned his name several years ago. One day recently he showed up at my door wanting to talk about books, knowing that having quite a few stories to tell was something we had in common. That's always a ticket inside.

"Let's talk about *this* book," I said, after a while. "The one I'm writing now. Imagine you're speaking to a person in Canada or the U.S.A., someone who's daydreaming about moving to México. Maybe it's someone who's actually decided to make the move, and is serious about looking for the right place to land. You've lived in San Miguel for twenty-five years. After all your travels around the world, what is it about this town that made it your firm choice?" We were sitting in my courtyard, edged by xeriscape plantings, organos cactus, and succulents of all shapes and sizes, many in flower.

He nodded for a while before he spoke. "It was and it is one of the most beautiful places I've ever been. Growing up in a little town in north Texas, Grandview, I didn't have much access to beauty. But it is here, and it's beautiful in a lot of different ways. I've met a lot of good people here from starting in '78—that was my first visit to San Miguel. Two gringo guys and I drove south from Matamoros, looking for adventure. I remember being up in the third floor of the Posada de las Monjas (an old hotel on Canal, just below the overpass), looking west and seeing the mountains. I guess I was twenty-eight years old. The room was reasonably priced; in fact it was cheap. I can remember one other time being in the smallest one they had. It cost about two dollars a night."

"What was remarkable about this town then?" Trying to connect it to what was happening in the U.S. at that time, I realized that this was during the middle of Jimmy Carter's term of office. The Soviets had just invaded Afghanistan.

"Well, it was foreign, but not too foreign. At the same time it makes me think about it that way now. From my house this morning on a three-mile walk I spoke to about twenty-five people. Most of them I know well enough to speak to because I'm on that route almost every day. (Jim Priest does not own a car.) Again, I'm coming from a small town in Texas, where you talk to everybody. If they're strangers they're not going to be strangers for long. One of the things I really enjoy involves older folks. I hung out with a bunch of older folks as a kid because that's what there was. It's that same sort of thing. People here are going about their everyday lives, counting tortillas, or whatever they're doing, and if they look up I give them a '*Buenos dias, Señora!*' You get a good smile back. I'm just a junkie for that."

"Do you find that this town is still cheap to live in?"

"It can be. For backpacking travellers to be cheap now you have to be creative, or go to the hostel and eat at home. Other than that, if you're just going to be here for a couple of days, maybe not. I saw a backpacker yesterday, but they don't get here much now because it's more expensive."

"What were you looking for when you settled here? Have you found it?"

"A comfortable, reasonably priced, good time. The good time was barely above comfort level back then. It was nice if it was comfortable too—I've always wanted at least basic comfort. Friends have also always been important to me. Some people say that, and you wouldn't know it by their actions, but people who are concerned about having friends take care of their friends. Back in 1978 here I remember meeting Pancho Villa #2. He seemed like an old guy, had a big black handlebar mustache. He sold postcards and calendars downtown. Over the years he was in a dozen different places. Just a classic guy. He always referred to women as *muñecas*, dolls. That didn't sit very well with me because I didn't look at things like that, but we had a good connection. I miss him now."

I asked whether #2 might really have been related to Pancho Villa, who died in 1923. Jim suggested that Villa had a lot of descendants all over México now. He was an active guy and women liked him. He had what we now call charisma.

"Was that kind of connectedness part of what you

were looking for here?"

"Not consciously, but it was important."

"How does the U.S. look to you now?" You never know what answer this will bring. Many people come here tossing a curse over their shoulder and never go back, and others return twice a year for family, for grandchildren, and shopping.

"My first take is that I'm glad I'm not living in the States, although I have a lot of friends there who greatly enjoy their lives. Since I first started traveling in the early 70s, and it was my trip to Europe after university, I hated to run into people at hostels who'd be badmouthing the U.S. It's even easier to do that now. But how the hell did you get enough money to put together living here? How many kids from Ethiopia or Guatemala can do that? It's all because of the U.S. and how it was set up. I was a product of that too. I don't usually involve myself in those conversations, but I'll hear people talking. They're on their first big trip and they're talking about how bad things are in the States. And it gets to be about how crappy everything else is with the economy and the government. I don't raise the issue anymore that if you didn't have an American passport, if you had been born in China, you'd be just one of a billion plus. Seems like the U.S. middle class is shrinking as it's growing in México. The biggest shopping mall in México is open now only forty miles from here. (The Antea Lifestyle Center, on the nearer edge of Querétaro.)

"What I see in the U.S. now is a lot of scary rednecks and they've all got guns. Friends of mine sent me some video of an art opening in downtown Fort Worth a couple of weeks ago with a guy showing up carrying an assault weapon—to an art opening! Fear does a lot of things."

In traveling throughout México for my most recent expat book, *Into the Heart of México*, I certainly encountered every degree of affection and antipathy toward the U.S. Being an American has also gotten more controversial over the years to people who aren't.

"What are some of the important ways San Miguel has changed during your tenure here?"

"Obviously it has way more cars and way more people. We've got a loop road around town now (the *libramiento*). And now we have Mega. I hope no one saw what they were planning on building there and gave them a go ahead. To me it's a big industrial building. It's not ugly but it's certainly not attractive." Mega is the big box supermarket where I shop for most things, other than what I get at specialty stores for artisanal cheeses or the organic market for fruits and vegetables. It does have an industrial look, but at least it's a long way from the colonial center. As for the design, I'm not sure what a neo-colonial big box supermarket would look like.

"Has the kind of person moving here also changed during the time you've been here?"

"Yes, I think so. In the seventies and eighties there were a lot more *vagabundos*. This was after the *On The Road* people, Ken Kesey and that Merry Pranksters bunch."

"On the psychedelic painted bus named *Further*," I suggested.

"They laid the groundwork for people like me to be able to get on a bus on the Méxican border with three or four hundred dollars and be here on that for a couple of weeks. Have a good time and go back home and tell stories about it. You hardly ever have backpackers here now; it's too expensive compared to southern México. At the same time, for those of us that have to pay attention to where our pesos go, that can be dealt with. There are places where you can eat a good lunch for fifty pesos ($4).

"Green exists here now, the green movement, and now we've got a couple of places that sell organic produce.

There are restaurants with vegetarian items on the menu. Now you can get decent coffee here. You used to get Sanka."

"What kind of person does best as an expat here?"

"In 2007 there were people on the shuttle to Leon who were by themselves and had it set up that they could look at a house on the way to the airport, and they bought it! Liberal, open, financially secure people are the ones who need to be here. They also need to understand *mañana*."

"So they've got to have the pace right. What are expats looking for here?"

"Presently I don't have any idea. I guess it's the same as me. Comfort, value, climate, personal enrichment, the arts, and good food. Some of the foreigners now, and a few of them are friends of mine, they don't have any contact with Mexicans. Other than the few that clean their house or do their garden."

"Staff."

"Right. The reason they communicate at all is because they have selected staff that is marginally bilingual."

"What kind of person would not do well moving here?"

"Conservatives who want their American or Canadian lives here. To me I look at the Civil List as a means of entertainment when you've got folks on there wondering where to get maple syrup and Oreo cookies. If that's your gig, you may be in the wrong place. You've got to be open to change and willing to accept San Miguel. If you're not an accepting person you're probably in the wrong place."

I took the word *conservative* to mean rigid in lifestyle and unwilling to change, because I've known a number of political conservatives who fit in very well here, although they're clearly in the minority. My estimate of Democrats among the American expat population is about 85%.

"What would you tell expats moving here that would

help them to adapt and settle in more easily?"

"Accept that you're a guest here. Treat everyone as you want to be treated and learn as much Spanish as you can, and use it. Poor to mediocre Spanish is a thousand times better than just speaking louder English."

CHAPTER 18

NIGHT LIFE

To repeat one of the questions I was asked several times as I talked with people at the house tour, "But what do people do here?" In other words, do the city fathers roll up the streets at eight o'clock?

Aside from strolling through those ancient streets at sunset and watching the passersby in the *jardín*, which I've addressed several chapter back, I decided to refer this question to Aarón Romo and Anne Nicolai.

Aarón is a bass player who studied both in México City and New York. Anne worked in public relations in Minneapolis until 2008, when, by her own account, she made "a positive, exciting change to a sunny place because I didn't like winter."

We met at Mama Mia, a bar and restaurant on Calle Umarán half a block from the *jardín*. At forty years old, it's the most seasoned watering hole in San Miguel. With a couple of side rooms and a rooftop lounge, the principal space is an interior courtyard holding a bandstand and bar, with dining tables that can be shifted off to one side to open the dance floor. Add tequila and some music and you have created an event. Nesting in the ficus trees are illuminated lanterns among strings of pin spots in tubes. The old stucco and worn stone door casings mark it as a survivor of the 1810 War of

Independence and every other conflict since. Like most buildings in *centro*, it was probably a house at one time.

We sat at a small table near the empty bandstand, away from the chatter and crunch of lunch guests. Once the waiter had left we talked. Aarón Romo is at once an intense but understated man of serious demeanor. In our early conversation he took my questions straight up and answered them from his long experience.

Anne is a trim blonde of average height, with long curly hair.

"Suppose you have a younger couple here in San Miguel visiting from out of town," I said. "They've never been here before, but they're not intimidated about being in México. Where would they go in the evening for some fun?"

"If they're in their twenties they're going to start at Don Taco Tequila, or right here at Mama Mia," Anne said. Don Taco Tequila is a highly rated eatery not far from where we sat, a block further away from the *jardín* on Hernández Macias.

"Or El Grito or Mint," added Aarón, "or Bezzito."

"What kind of music would they hear at those places?"

Anne shrugged. "It's just recorded music with a D.J."

"What are the live group places?"

"Tio Lucas and Mama Mia have live music every day. It's going to be a jazz trio at Tio Lucas. At Mama Mia on Monday, Aarón plays with a Latin jazz trio. On Tuesday he and I host bilingual karaoke at la Choperia on Canal." Anne also mentioned Mi Casa inside the Instituto Allende, and VC and Friends on Hernández Macias.

"Tell me about the karaoke process. I've never done it or seen it. Are there other clubs that also feature it?"

"We also do it Fridays at The Beer Company, and we start early so we get a real mix of expats and Mexicans, younger people, visitors and locals. You can also find it at Mama Mia on Wednesdays and Thursdays."

"What do people have to do to sing on stage here?"

"They can sign up and choose their song. We also have remote microphones and you can even sing from your table if you like."

"Do you have the music, or do they bring theirs? How does that work?"

"I own all the music for our show. It's called Karaoke Annie."

"What kind of material do you bring to this?"

"I have the largest collection of music in San Miguel. It's 100% legal, and that's unique. I take pride in that. It's everything from rap to hip-hop and pop, and music back to wartime. I've got Broadway show tunes."

"So if my mother is in town and she wants to sing *I Had a Dream* from *Les Miserables*, the one Susan Boyle did on Britain's Got Talent, could you set her up for that?" It had suddenly occurred to me that much of the vocal part of that program was the equivalent of network karaoke.

"Yes, and we often do. It's wonderful."

"Would you characterize this as a hopping town?" They both hesitated a bit on this question.

"A lot of the younger set from México City will come here and they are lined up outside Bezzito, or El Grito, or Mint."

"What else do you have for the range of music offered here?"

"We have a variety in the clubs. Salsa and blues are the strongest ones right now," said Aarón. "Our group also plays salsa at Hotel Hacienda de Guadalupe two nights a week."

"There's also a strong community of salsa dancers here," Anne added.

"Previously, around fifteen years ago, it was rock. I was doing it five nights a week back then."

"Have you worked with Doc Severinsen here?"

"Not yet, but he recently moved back to San Miguel and asked me to join his band."

Doc Severinsen has lived in San Miguel for years, and often plays with local groups when he's not touring.

"Do you write music yourself?"

"Yes."

"What kind of things do you write?"

"I prefer rock, because when I began playing that's what I started with. But I like other rock-influenced music, too. I'm also an arranger."

"Reading this, my readers are going to wonder how old you two are. You don't have to say."

"My birthday," said Anne, shaking this off, "is a week from today and I'll be 52."

"I'm 39," said Aarón.

"We met at karaoke," she added.

No surprise there.

"Suppose I'm a musician and I'm looking to expand my horizons from what's happening with my career in the States. Would this be a good place to come down and try to break into the music scene? How would a person do that?"

"You'd go to the piano bar," Anne said.

"Or you could come to Mama Mia," said Aarón. "It depends on where you're coming from. The Cuban musicians come here to this club. They all know each other."

"What if I'm not Cuban? What if I'm Norwegian?" Apparently, from the list of Scandinavian sounding names that quickly followed, that was not a problem. "Is it hard to break in? Do I have to know somebody?"

Aarón didn't answer this directly. "For me as a bass

player, it's both a curse and a blessing. There aren't many of us in San Miguel, and the ones there are get all the gigs. Like in salsa, I am *the* bass player. In blues or in rock, somebody else gets all those gigs. That covers it. San Miguel is not a great place for live bands now, not like it used to be."

"Is it your sense that the traffic at the clubs, the ones you work at, is down over the last four or five years?

"I don't know, but it is different."

"Let's say you have a couple down here from Pough-keepsie. They're in their forties and they want to go out and do a little dancing with a live group. How do they research where to go? I mean starting cold. Say they've never been here and they know next to nothing about it."

"Well, in Atención. The Que Pasa section each week," Anne responded.

"They should go to Atención and get the name of the place," said Aarón, "and then go to the Facebook page for an accurate idea."

"Anything else for someone thinking of moving here?"

"Just a little more about the piano bar," said Anne. "It's called La Noche, right across from the Angela Peralta Theater at the bottom of Mesones. They have an open mike for talented people. If you're good and you know you're good, you can go there and bring your instrument. Then you hand your business card out to people. You get to know other musicians, and sometimes they need substitutes. At other times there are *bohemias*, too, which are jam sessions. You bring whatever instrument you play."

Bringing whatever instrument you play might be true of all of us coming down here, I thought. Music can be a metaphor for the performance we favor in life. My own keyboard fronts a laptop. Choose your stage and your material. In her karaoke show, Anne has a load of it to choose from, and it's all legal.

CHAPTER 19

DATING

There are numerous jokes circulating about dating in San Miguel and although people kept offering me the latest one, I'm not going to use any of them. At first I thought I'd list them all, but the conversation that follows turned out to be quite substantive and full of insights, and I don't want to begin this frivolously. Single people of both genders head to San Miguel with a variety of expectations. For those who haven't lived here for some period of time it's hard to imagine how they could be realistic. Single—not to say available—women outnumber men by a large margin. As in any imbalance of that kind, there will be no easy solution for women looking for a partner.

In writing this chapter I'm not going to present a solution for finding a good mate here, although there are some ways to explore the scene. As with any town, volunteering for NGOs is a way to meet people. There is also a newcomer's gathering once a month that can get you connected. Church groups are also a good way. On Wednesdays there's Lady's Night at Hank's on Hidalgo half a block from the *jardín*. Attending Spanish classes has always been one of the best ways to meet people here.

The story below is about one couple that succeeded, and embedded in it are some ideas about attitude and preconceptions that can be used by others. It's unique, just as all of these stories are.

I wanted to talk about dating with Judith Jenya and Mark Johaningsmeir because I knew they had met here in México and gotten married within the last few years. While it is the story of two expats, there will also be other stories of expats successfully connecting with Mexicans, but that is rarer and more often happens in towns with a smaller expat community.

Mark grew up in Waukegan, Illinois, went to college in Iowa as an English major, and after several years in the work force, went on to attend a seminary in St. Paul. He was ordained as a United Methodist pastor, got married and had two children.

But after twenty-five years serving the church, a stroke ended his career, and he moved to Guanajuato, our capital city, to begin a new life. Four years later he was divorced.

Judith Jenya comes from a diverse and more complex background. The daughter of European refugees, she grew up in California and first saw San Miguel as a teenager on a visit with her mother. The image of this town and its art scene stayed with her as she went to school at the University of California at Berkeley, Harvard, and the University of Hawaii. She has worked as an attorney, art teacher, art therapy psychotherapist, and a humanitarian activist. She has been the recipient of many awards for her public service activities throughout the world. She is also a published poet and writer, and regularly exhibits her photography and painting.

As we sat in the rear patio of their house over coffee, I plunged right in. "I've been told this is a good town to write in, to paint in, or to be an actor, but is it a good town to be single in if you want to have a social life?"

"I can answer that question because when I moved

here I was single, and I remained single for four years, until October of 2010, when I met Mark." Judith had moved to San Miguel in 2006.

"I was very interested in dating and finding a partner. There is a dearth of reasonable, eligible men here, but there is not a dearth of *unreasonable*, eligible men, many of whom are lacking in one of the following: money, brains, health, sanity, and the ability to be in a relationship. There are a number of loner-type men here, or losers, or extreme introverts, or people who just like being on their own. That really limits the field. There are also a lot of people who would not be good partners because they're in bad shape in one way or another. The few dates that I had with men I met randomly here at an art opening, or in the *jardín*, or at a party, to me they were not the right sort of people by any stretch of the imagination."

"Had you started by defining for yourself in specific terms what you were looking for?"

"Actually, each time I met somebody it became cleaer what that was."

"It sharpened the criteria," added Mark.

"So what I did for those four years was online dating in the U.S. or Canada. When I had a conversation going and the person seemed sort of interesting, I'd say, 'Why don't you come down to San Miguel for a visit?' I had ten such visits."

"That's an interesting twist on this," I said, "that you were shopping long distance." And on the surface, that did make a lot of sense. If you weren't finding what you were looking for already here, then draw someone in.

"I moved here when I was sixty-five, so the people I was corresponding with were roughly in my age category. Many of them were trying to figure out what they wanted to do, or whether they wanted to retire somewhere else, so that San Miguel seemed interesting enough that they'd come down. None of those ten people were of any interest to me, once I met them, as it turned out."

"What did you find were their principal shortcomings? Was there a trend?"

"A trend. Well, some of them understated their physical limitations. I had always emphasized to them that I hoped they were healthy and could walk, because this can be a difficult town to get around in."

"And many of them arrived on a gurney with a traveling nurse and an IV," I suggested.

"Something like that," Judith said, stifling a laugh. "Or, one of the things that happens with online dating, or in talking to them on Skype, is that they learn about you, and if they're interested in pursuing a relationship with you, then they tailor who they are to meet that. It sounds as if you have a lot in common, until you actually meet this person, and then you discover that's not who they really are. I don't think any amount of Skyping or emailing gets you where you need to be in terms of knowing somebody else. I thought my basic criteria were fairly simple. They had to be reasonably healthy, bright, capable of having an interesting conversation, not too emotionally damaged to have a relationship, and not on their fifth wife, although many people are."

"And solvent," suggested Mark, dryly.

"That one was a little bit touchy also. Some people came down, and I was living on Social Security, but I had bought this house when I came. (Mortgages are unusual here.) I did a lot of things to earn extra money. Some people came down and recognized that I could use a greater income, and that was offered to me. I had this one guy say, 'Well, you know, I have so much per month in retirement and I'd be happy to be here with you and we can share it.'"

"That was very nice, but that wasn't the only thing

I wanted, to share somebody's retirement. So I think that as you're older and trying to find a lifetime partner, as opposed to just dating, we all come with so much baggage, things that can trip us up or get in our way, that unless people have worked on themselves somewhat and have some self-awareness by this point in life, they're not good partner material, because they don't understand themselves well enough to be in a relationship that works."

"That's what you mean by worked on themselves?"

"Yes, spent time learning about themselves, and the intrinsic things that are important to them. Have a spiritual life and a real understanding of who they are. Not who they wish they were, but who they really are, their limitations and their strengths, and that they can share those with another person. That is a tough issue."

"Have you been married before?"

She nodded slowly. "I was married for twenty years, and I have two grown children and a grandchild. I was one of those who got married at twenty-two. I was married into what in America was considered a great marriage, but it wasn't great for me."

"I wasn't going to ask this, but I'd like to enter your ages in this chapter so that the reader gets a clearer look at where we are. Age is a factor in this discussion, more so than if we were all thirty."

"I'm seventy-three," said Judith.

"And I'm sixty-five," said Mark.

"I don't care," said Judith, "that's the age I am. I don't think it's the age so much as being youthful in your outlook on life. I look a lot younger than I am."

This is true. Judith Jenya is a tall woman with a round, expressive face that displays a wide range of emotion. Her capacity for humor is clear in her eyes, and from any distance

226

she could easily be the same age as Mark. Her hair is chestnut, and whether from nature or choice, none of it is gray.

"So that's the background," I said. "That process of online dating, which was meant to substitute for meeting eligible people here that didn't materialize very well, that didn't work out either, after ten meetings with men on your short list."

"I would've continued with it because it was so entertaining, to say the least. But then I met Mark. Meanwhile I had been doing a lot of other things, like having an art exhibition every year. The biggest one I ever had was in Guanajuato, in September of 2010. Mark came to the closing. I thought he was really attractive. He was fun to talk with and sexy. He seemed like a *decent* man. That's an important criterion for me. Being a decent, honorable person."

"And Mark, you were living then in Guanajuato."

"I moved there at virtually the same time that Judith moved here."

"And you moved there after a stroke that virtually ended your career in the ministry."

"Yes. I had the stroke in 2001. I went back to work way too soon and kept at it for two more years as my health deteriorated to the point where I just couldn't. I went on medical disability, did lots of therapy, and I had always had a fantasy about living in México. Because every winter both from the time I lived in Minnesota and when I lived in the Denver area, we did winter vacations in México, and just loved it."

"You already knew Guanajuato."

"I had visited Guanajuato, and my ex and I tried it out for a couple of months, and decided that was going to be a good place."

"His ex is bilingual, so that helps," added Judith.

"We moved in 2006, and I just felt like I had died and

gone to Heaven. But the marriage was not in Heaven. So that was getting worse, and at the same time my life was expanding. I was more interested in that expansion of life than what felt like a constricting and unhealthy relationship. So she moved out in the spring of 2010, and when she wanted later to get back together, I said no, this is too good. I want a divorce. It was early summer when that conversation took place, and it was the end of September when I had been back in the States for six weeks, and just got back home and noticed there were some things going on at this gallery. Judith was there when I arrived and hardly anybody else was."

"It was very late when he showed up," Judith added.

"It was the last hour of the last day of her exhibit, and we got to talking. We pulled up a couple of chairs and sat swapping stories of our lives, and finding little points of contact amid all kinds of very obvious differences in ethic background, differences in religious background, but in common we had values around social justice, fairness, and we got into political things very quickly. There we found a great deal of similarity in where we stood."

"Did you think of yourself as available at that time?"

"At that point in my mind, the marriage was already over. We were separated, and she was still living in town, but I considered myself as single. So we had this interesting conversation. I found Judith fascinating. It was hard to believe because of all the stories she was telling about her life. But since then I've discovered she was telling the truth. So she went off to visit family in the States two days after we met, and we emailed a bit during that time. She came back and we got tickets to a couple of events at the Cervantino Festival. (A cultural festival held each fall in Guanajuato that honors Miguel de Cervantes.) By the second date, we were together, we were a couple. Just amazing!"

"Imagine now a person in Peoria, reading this. She's unattached and she's trying to think of, among other aspects of San Miguel, what she might get going socially if she came down here. What would you tell her? After your experience, what should she do if she wanted to meet someone? Is there a great answer to that or not?"

"I don't think there is a great answer to that," said Judith. "But I think there's a great attitude you can have, which is, first of all, to be accepting of yourself as you are. Secondly, when you meet somebody, accept that person for who they are, as opposed to how they fit into your category. So for me, I think that's what enabled me to have a relationship with Mark. It was that I made the decision that I was going to explore this man and the possibilities with complete acceptance, as opposed to judgment and criticism. For me, that made all the difference in the world. A lot of women have asked me, 'How did you manage to do that, how did you find somebody? I haven't found anybody.' I said 'Well, how open are you to accepting somebody as they are?'"

It will be no surprise to the reader if I was seeing a therapist's insights in this process, combined with a lot of realism and common sense.

"Now, you come from a Jewish background, and you, Mark, are Methodist."

He nodded with an ironic smile, but Judith went on.

"And my parents were European refugees, leftwing socialists. That was the environment I grew up with in California, and in Hawaii. I had never even been to the Midwest. It's like some terra incognita if you've lived on the coast."

"It's like Siberia in Judith's mind," said Mark.

"I can see that," I said.

"Mark, for me, was exotic. I had never met anyone from the Midwest. He was a minister who had this normal life, a Norman Rockwell upbringing. Had I met him earlier in my life I would not have been remotely interested, because I was living a very interesting 'out there in the world' life. So partly, it's me now, it's about where I am. I'm not interested in the wild adventures that I used be interested in."

"This is partly about the time of your life," I said.

"And knowing and accepting myself better, and doing the same with him. That's not something I was very good at before. A lot of single women who come here have been very independent like me, and very competent, and done their solo life well. So giving up the kind of intense autonomy that comes with that and choosing to make this a priority is part of how you can have a sustaining relationship anywhere you are. That was a conscious decision that I made."

I paused for a moment before taking up a new thread, because that final statement resonated with me as a critical one.

"In spite of the divergence of your religious backgrounds, you have both found an overlap in the value systems you share. That's part of what makes this work."

"It works very well, and we're respectful of each other's backgrounds."

"Mark doesn't try to baptize you when you're not looking."

"Not when I *am* looking, anyway. I'm more interested than Mark is at this point in anything of organized religion. Occasionally I go to Jewish things and he goes with me, and we were at a spiritual Shabbat dinner at the Jewish Center here two weeks ago and we drove somebody home who's going to be a neighbor on the next street, who is newly arrived here, and he happens to be Jewish. This guy says, about Mark and me, 'Oh, it's so nice to have another Jewish family on the street.' Mark, I thought, has come a long way." Laughter followed. Mark is an angular blond guy with a trim

Scandinavian build. If he hadn't said he was born in Wauke-gan, I would've guessed Minnesota.

"Are the single women here mostly looking for some-one, or are they content to live with a minimal dating pool here? Perhaps you can't generalize, although you certainly did test the waters for yourself."

"First of all there's a very strong community of wom-en here, so if you're single and a woman and an artist, say, there's a whole group of other single woman artists. People get together and do things with that community. I think many of them are not interested in having a long-term relationship. For many women of my generation, having been married meant that your needs and interests were subordinate to those of your husband either professionally or in some other way. Now that they don't have to be married to somebody, and they're not raising children anymore, they can pursue their own interests on their own time and not have to accommo-date anyone. That is a *huge* benefit for many women here. So they may want some companionship, but many are not look-ing for a long-term relationship. One of the things people ask me is, 'How could you possibly arrange for somebody to come into your house, your space, and let them live there. How can you manage that?' For me it hasn't been that hard, which surprises me."

"It has to be partly about how territorial you are," I suggested.

"Yes, and partly about the decisions one makes, like is it more important for me to have all the space I had before, or is it more important to find space for this man I love."

"How has that been for you, Mark, coming into this space? Look at that issue from the flip side."

"The move from my rental home in Guanajuato to San Miguel was extreme. I was living in a fairly large flat.

My ex had taken fifty percent or more of the furniture. The place was looking pretty Spartan. Judith's space is all color and movement. If you had walked through here a month ago, every square inch of the walls was covered with framed photos and paintings that she'd done. I had a lot of books and bookcases that I'd brought with me. It was interesting to make the visual switch between that nearly empty apartment and being here. I spent the first three years looking around this house and discovering new things on the walls. I love being in this space."

I also wanted to look at some nuts and bolts issues that young people don't usually have to think about.

"If you're connecting with someone and you're both older, what are the arguments to get married or not?" Judith took this one.

"I think the reason people don't get married is that they're worried about finances, about incurring financial liabilities for the other person, they want to leave everything to their own kids, or their kids are upset about the idea. I know people who don't get married because of that. They're worried about being burdened with someone else's ill health. Those are reasons people give, or it's too conventional, or they've already done that. In our case, that isn't how we felt about marriage. We have shared and pooled everything. It has not been a problem.

"I still find every single day a complete wonder that we're together. It's amazing that we found one another. It was just by the slightest of circumstances. If Mark hadn't shown up during those last minutes we never would've crossed paths. For some odd reason we're very happy and well suited to each other at this point in our lives."

"Life is good. Life is just incredibly good. I'm so in love with Judith and our life together."

This is no blueprint for romance. A lot of it was, as both Judith and Mark acknowledge, pure chance, as it often is under more normal circumstances. I did not ever think that they were going to provide a formula of how to come down here and get connected. This is not a roadmap of how it's done, although it offers many insights into how to approach it and think about it productively.

I have cast this mostly from a woman's perspective, since we have so many more single women than men here in the expat population. But what if we turn this around? From what Judith has said about the character of much of the female expatriate population, what an opportunity awaits the confident, insightful, single man looking for a partner in a meaningful relationship. I'm not talking about cruising. If I wanted to meet a woman who already had a rewarding life, who had amazing things to offer, but lacked desperation, I would come down here in a heartbeat.

I am most fortunate to already have that connection, but if I did not…

CHAPTER 20

GAY SAN MIGUEL

In my travels around México as I worked on *Into the Heart of México*, I came across a surprising number of gay couples living in out of the way places. Surprising because I assumed most gays would congregate in areas with more of an international flavor, places with a strong expat community like San Miguel, Lake Chapala, or México City, places that were therefore less xenophobic and more laid back about lifestyle differences. What I found instead was that gays were scattered throughout this country, and while I spent some effort in trying to discover whether México had some special appeal for them, I can't say that I was able to cast much light on that aspect of it.

San Miguel has a strong gay community of long standing. The legalization of same sex unions in México City in 2010 has not only added a new dimension to gay pride here, but a sense of engagement with this community and their adopted country as well. On a Wednesday morning in July I hooked up with two old friends from Dallas, Lisa Tyson and Laurie Sandefer.

Both are in their later forties now. Laurie is a painter with a Ph.D. in aesthetics. Lisa had a career as an attorney that placed her on the fast track to being corporate counsel in a Fortune 500 company, a track she stepped off when they moved to San Miguel eight years ago.

They share a spacious two story black and white house in the Guadiana neighborhood. We sat inside because there were workers busy in the courtyard. As with other people I've spoken with in this project, I had sent them the interview questions in advance to give them time to think about them and even bat them around before we talked.

"Does San Miguel have a special charm that appeals to the gay community?"

"We talked about all your questions when we got them, and we really don't think so," Lisa said. "I can't think of anything that is particularly charming (to gays) in ways that wouldn't be the same to anyone. We asked a couple of our gay men friends, Charles and Rod, about that and they agreed."

"There's really not the same kind of gay community here that there is in the States," added Laurie. "In the big cities up north there are far bigger gay communities and much more going on in that respect. That would never be a reason anyone would find San Miguel interesting, because we don't have that here."

"How did you choose this town?"

"Well, specifically San Miguel," began Laurie, "I had a Spanish tutor in Dallas, and she had lived in México for several years. When we said we wanted to move to México, we told her we had no idea where. She said, 'Try San Miguel, it's beautiful, I think you'll love it. At least make your start there, because your Spanish sucks so bad you won't make it anywhere else.' She really did say that. We had no idea. We'd never been in any of the colonial towns, only the beach places. We came and visited it and we fell in love with it.

"When was that?"

"We came the first time in 2004."

"If you two hadn't come down here as a couple, would you still have come alone, and would you have expected to meet someone here?"

"That's a hard question," Laurie said, "Because we've been together for so long."

"It's so hard to imagine what I would have done without Laurie, but if something happened to Laurie now, I would stay. But I know that lots of other gay people come down here and find someone. It's totally possible."

Laurie picked up this thread. "We were also talking with Rod and Charles about the differences for gay guys and for lesbians. They think that because so many people do move down here as couples, it can be challenging to find a dating scene because there aren't any really gay bars, and not really gay cliques. Most people move down here as a couple. They said that for men it can be even more challenging to find someone they want to date."

"But, we have lots of friends who have," added Lisa.

"I think it's just the lack of a clearly delineated community."

"Where you can go fishing."

"In my previous book, *Into the Heart of Mexico: Expatriates Find Themselves off the Beaten Path*, I came across what seemed to me quite a high proportion of gay couples in places you wouldn't necessarily expect; I didn't anyway. I was thinking that gay people are more drawn to sophisticated places, places that might have more of an international flavor, as this place does. Yet I found gay couples all over in populations with few other expats."

"We've said before," said Laurie, "and this is after being here full time for over eight years, that if for some reason we couldn't live in San Miguel, we would for sure move further south, rather than head anywhere north. If we couldn't afford to, that would be our choice, to go deeper into Latin America. We would have more confidence to do that at this point. I can see us living in a mostly Mexican town. But we never want to leave here."

"Does this mean that México tolerates or encourages a more forthright display of same gender preferences, even in areas that are not trendy or sophisticated? This is a densely Catholic country, and very traditional in most of its values, yet there's a tolerance here that some people would not expect to find."

"I don't know about the people you came across in your travels," said Lisa, "but I do think it would still be a lot easier, other things being equal, to live in a small remote place in México rather than anywhere in the U.S."

"As a gay couple."

"For sure," said Laurie. "We have never had any issues here. And we asked our men friends and they said, no, they haven't had any discrimination. One of them is Mexican and the other is American. They've been together for several years."

"The culture," said Lisa, "is so accepting, but not just of the gay issue. The religious part and the secular part are so separate in many ways. So, it's been my experience in the San Miguel culture that they really don't care about your sexuality, where you're from, what you do. They care about your character and your integrity. So it seems like it's easier to live an "out" lifestyle here in San Miguel. I can't speak for other parts of México, but it certainly seems that way. I would expect that if you did run into trouble here it would be more likely to come from an American."

"Absolutely."

"You think of yourself as being mostly out."

"Entirely out."

"Of course with México making same sex marriage legal," said Laurie, "in 2010, and us getting married in México City, the government and people here are so supportive, versus what's still going on in the States. The judge who spoke at our wedding was an older woman. We'd never met her. She was so pro-love. She was probably sixty-five or seventy years old. Anyway, with that experience, after years of other kinds of experiences, we just can't say enough about how we feel embraced here."

"Can you think of one gay person we know here who's not out?" asked Lisa.

"No, not one. When DOMA (The Defense of Marriage Act), a key provision of which, allowing states to discriminate legally against same sex people married under the laws of the other states, was overruled by the Supreme Court in the States in September, 2013, one of our housekeepers happened to be here while we were watching the announcement on TV, and she saw it. We were crying. We had a much bigger reaction than we thought we would. But she hugged us and told us that her sister was gay. She told us about the struggle within her family, but now the family completely accepts her sister."

"This is an extremely conservative, traditional culture," I said, "and I assume a lot of the resistance to civil unions for gay people in the States comes from the Bible Belt, another old, traditional culture. Yet the attitudes are so different. I'm not sure why."

"I see it across every aspect of that culture," said Lisa.

"In general, the Mexican culture seems to be less judgmental in the sense of things like, Oh, Uncle Juan died of alcoholism just because he loved to drink so much. This is said with no criticism implied. Or, Aunt so and so died of diabetes because she just loved sweets. It's a totally different approach than saying that they deserved to die because they took pleasure in what killed them. Those statements are not something you would commonly hear in the U.S."

"Within the population of people who move to

Mexico, do you think there is there a larger percentage of gay people?"

"I don't think so," said Lisa. "We don't know any more gay people here than we did in the States, that's for sure."

"I haven't seen that," said Laurie. "We've been in the business of renting our home and dabbled a little in real estate. Charles, our friend, is a realtor and we have some other realtor friends. There are a lot of both gay and straight realtors, and it doesn't seem like they talk about more gay people moving here."

"No, and you know what I think? This might have something to do with the lifestyle we all live when we get here, including you. I don't know what you did in Minnesota, maybe you were busy working and you didn't have time to go around and interview people and look at that."

"I surely wasn't writing books like this one there."

"I think that here most of us lead such a different life now than we led in the States," said Lisa, "and we're just more aware of that, like who your neighbor is. In Dallas we didn't know our neighbors. You got in your car and went to work, and you knew the people you worked with."

"But you don't know whether some of the people you work with are gay or not because they're too scared to come out of the closet. At least you didn't back then."

"I think it's partly a function of time and the world we live in now, and also a function of the way we act with each other here. We know more about each other, or we know each other in different ways."

"To me, as I work on books like this, it seems like there's a greater gay presence here and in México as a whole, and I keep hearing that is not true."

"I have not found that to be true at all," said Lisa.

"Maybe what I'm experiencing is that I was not doing

anything like that in Minnesota, and maybe my circuit back then didn't take me through the same circles."

"Right, because you were focused on other things in your life at that time."

I began to see that the issue might not be the way I expressed it, but rather, on the Minnesota end, years ago, there simply had been a lack of contact. We lived in an upper middle class neighborhood surrounded by other families with children. We had children at home ourselves then.

"I really think so," said Laurie. "Also, people who have the guts to pick up their lives and move are usually a little more open-minded or daring. If you had your typical life, whatever that meant for you in the United States, then to pick up and move I think does take a special person, although what that means can vary. It might be financial or political. When you land in a foreign country you're more likely to be open to things. If you're daring enough to move to a foreign country, you probably have different values when you get to that country...Homophobic people wouldn't make it very long here in the social world of San Miguel."

"Most gay people," added Lisa, "do not have children. A lot of the gay people we know here are young, and had accumulated the money they needed to come here at an early age, and I think that's partly a function of not having to raise kids."

"In terms of acceptance of gay people here," I said, "there's a long tradition of toleration of other people's lifestyle and habits. Is there any more to it than that?"

"I don't think so,' said Laurie, "except that it's not just tolerance, because there's that gigantic example of making gay marriage legal at a national level. That's proactive, and it goes beyond just tolerance."

"So let's talk about marriage then. I wonder if the

whole view of marriage in our culture is changing, and marriage is no longer compulsory in the way it once was. There is the option of people living together unmarried and having children, if they want to have children, whether they're in a conventional or a gay relationship. Perhaps the whole marriage idea is opening outward, becoming more elastic, which may be partly responsible for the fact that you can get married now in México City as a same gender couple. Do you see the opportunity that you took to get married as part of a broader opening out of the institution?"

"Being married to us," said Laurie, "in a traditional sense, was never something we were activists for. I mean we think everyone should be able to be married. The way our decision to get married started was that we were at our lawyer's office talking about the complicated issues of estates and real estate that gay people have to think about that straight people don't. It's more difficult here when you're not married and not related. She said to us, 'You know what would make things a lot easier for you two is if you got married.' We were both shocked. This was in April of 2010, and México had just passed the law in March. We had no idea. People ask us, who proposed to who, and we tell them that our lawyer proposed to us. We hopped in the cab afterward, and we said, do you want to? Yup." She nodded vigorously.

"Then it took on a whole different aspect," added Lisa.

"Once we knew it was possible, we couldn't wait to get married, not only for the logistical reasons, but also for a whole side of things that we had never imagined."

"Even if you don't care about all that," added Lisa, "the legal and financial benefits of being married far outweigh the costs."

"So those are the mechanics of it," I said, "and they're very important, elements that conventionally married people don't even think about because they take them for granted, like the absence of estate tax when passing assets to a spouse. But let's go on to the emotional component. What doors opened for you as you rode in that cab going back?"

"First of all," Lisa said, "being in a country we love so much, giving us permission to get married, we felt that much more accepted and welcome. Since we were at the early stages of when this became available, people in the wedding business weren't used to it and we were worried about that. I hoped a gay wedding wasn't going to be weird for them. But it was just lovely. We had an all female mariachi band from México City. It was the feeling that your society, your culture, the people you're around daily are happy for you and you get celebrated like everybody else does."

"Is part of this about conferring legitimacy on relationships that society has frowned upon in the past? Or is it more an affirmation that you weren't used to or even expecting?"

"I think part of it is legitimacy," Lisa said.

"I don't know if it's legitimacy," said Laurie. "From my early adulthood I was always philosophically against the institution of marriage, because of its historical roots, with the woman being considered chattel. So all that time I was asking why is it necessary. Yet, we're all human beings, and if someone acknowledges you as a couple, for your wedding anniversary or your birthday, it feels good to be known in a joyful way. So in that sense it is legitimacy, although we didn't need anybody to legitimize our love or our feelings."

"Am I right in calling that affirmation?"

"I think so. It's just being known, and being able to be known whoever you are. Like if you're sitting down having a drink with someone you want to be able to have a nice, fun, honest conversation about what you're doing that day. What you like and what you don't like. In that way, it's absolutely affirmation.

"Emotionally it was the realization of the juxtaposition of how it felt to be gay in the United States, and how lovely the experience has been here. Realizing how much it sucked there. We loved our lives there, but the oppression, you get so used to it, that when DOMA was overturned, given our experiences here of the last eight years, we just felt so grateful. We've been so lucky on this end."

"To shift gears just a bit, is there a gay nightlife scene here?"

"Well, since we go to bed about nine, we don't know. We asked our friends, and they said no. All the late night bar hopping, like at El Grito, they said it's very mixed, gay and straight."

"Well, we did go out a lot when we first came here," added Lisa.

"Of course, being a couple already, you were never out looking to connect with someone."

"Besides it would be single gay men out late at night trying to find someone, more than women would."

At that point I wasn't sure anymore what I had expected when I started this conversation. Perhaps that it was going to be focused on the nightclub scene here, bar hopping and hooking up, although I knew that Lisa and Laurie were a committed couple of long standing. This was more about the fundamental otherness that has been used to characterize gay members of our society in the States, how the laws discriminated against their relationships in direct and harmful ways, and how living in México brought a kind of release from that, just as it does in so many other areas. This again goes back to the *Release into Freedom* that I discussed in the opening chapter.

I left Lisa and Laurie's house in the *colonia* Guadiana

with the sense of having stepped onto and shared their path for a while. They had made me aware of how little I had done that in the past, and of how my own rather enclosed background made me think there were far more gays here than elsewhere, when the principal difference was mainly in my own expanded awareness. The conversation changed both my focus and my point of view. I have said this before, but writing is like teaching. In the process of informing others we instruct ourselves. The author is the first beneficiary of the book he writes.

CHAPTER 21

ARE WE THERE YET?

Whether I'm writing a nonfiction account of the expat experience, or the next volume of the San Miguel mystery series, *place* is always an important character in these narratives. In this book in particular, it anchors our exploration of the expat lifestyle. Yet, no matter how flawless our Spanish, how thorough our grasp of Mexican manners and customs, how enthusiastic our participation in the local fiestas and cultural events, we will always remain in some respects an outsider.

Perhaps we are a bit like the Lithuanian great uncle we recall from childhood, a man whose tea and tobacco-stained mustache was always too big and droopy, whose footing was never quite certain, whose ways were often opaque, and whose eagerness to please never fully made up for the disconnect between his distant history and our more recent one. Even as we welcomed him to our gatherings, his well-meaning presence always made us slightly uncomfortable and we could only fully relax once he left. Integration and acclimatization take time, and usually one generation at a minimum. I can recall relatives on my mother's side who sprinkled sugar on their lettuce, and on my father's side who poured vinegar on their cabbage. And they were born in the United States, although their grandparents were not.

I was about halfway through my travels across México, working on my book about expats living in out-of-the-way
places, when I experienced an unexpected shift in perspective.
Suddenly I saw myself, not as an American simply living in
México, a person who had chosen one location over another
without giving it any great significance as a change in *status*,
but as an immigrant, although much different in some ways
than that Lithuanian great uncle. Let me define immigrant
here as a person who has obtained permanent legal status in
his new country and is not going back, except for family visits
and shopping.

Those differences from the uncle's position, however,
mask a certain similarity in our dilemma. If we have made the
effort to get to know and mix with our neighbors, we will be
invited to Mexican family or perhaps business celebrations,
but we will probably feel like a wallflower, smiling too much
and wondering whether some of their delicious macaroni
salad is still stuck between our teeth. We will be careful not to
drink too much in an attempt to loosen up, although Mexican
manners will require that no one comment on it if we do. We
will laugh a bit too hard at our host's jokes, even when we
don't fully understand them. Overall, the sense of disconnect
of background and manners will be the same to us as to our
Mexican friends. Perhaps once we are gone they will feel they
have done their duty and can let their hair down, and perhaps
so will we.

This position is neither no man's land nor comfort
zone, but somewhere between, where maps are outdated and
landmarks rare. This may be why most expats prefer to live in
a community with an established expat component. We may
occasionally pick up an unfriendly look on the street and realize we are minorities here, and if we are white, that's usually an unaccustomed place to be. What may not be clear for

some time is that it also has another dimension. It is that while we are far from being a perfect fit here, neither can we go home again.

Of course I have watched with regret the cars of friends and neighbors, loaded with their dogs and luggage, disappear over the horizon headed north, never to return. These are people who, often for reasons of health, have come to believe they will do better in the U.S. or Canada. And that may be true. But I cannot help imagining the coming trials of reentry as well. Like a diver coming up from the bottom in stages to decompress and avoid the bends, I worry that they will have the same kind of risk as they try to work México out of their blood. Even if they locate the exact hole they once occupied in that peg board culture across the border, and slide back into it with a sigh of relief, they will find it has subtly changed in their absence. The edges are somehow rougher now and their skin chafes as they shift about trying to locate the kind of fit they once enjoyed.

Things may look reassuringly the same, but they have lost the *comfort* of their former place.

This is because of a condition that has come over them gradually during their residence here. The northern culture does not look the same from outside as from within. If you have lived south of the border for a while, your point of view has literally changed by degree. Part of this is being immersed in a culture of people who have always known things about their neighbor to the north that we don't, because that neighbor is us. Looking in the mirror may give us a sense of some of the detail, but the overall picture we have is not what our Mexican neighbor sees.

The bottom line is this: we cannot go home again to the place we recall so well, because now *we know too much*. That former homeland can only be inhabited by people more innocent and trusting than we are now. Like a tightrope walker working without a net, we find ourselves performing a balancing act that offers no resolution on either end. We are caught between what we once were and what we would like to be, and both are slightly beyond our present grasp.

This is the irony of the expatriate experience. Simply put, it is a condition neither here nor there, a phrase often used to describe something that is irrelevant, a situation that doesn't matter, but this status is fundamental to our new life.

So, are we there yet? No, and we will never be there in the sense of reaching a destination. But it turns out that the expat status is one of the most rewarding conditions to be in—that of the perpetual pilgrim, one who never reaches the end of the road, one whose days are filled with new experiences, challenges, opportunities for growth and development. It is a journey without signposts, and like life itself, it is not often a condition of equilibrium or of peace.

Even more than that, it is not journey's end.

CHAPTER 22

IT'S NOT FOR EVERYONE

B y now it will be clear that México should not be regarded as a cheaper version of the United States or
Canada, one with better winter weather and fresher
tortillas. It is not a country where the stack of dollars that
delivered you solidly into the middle class back home will
now make you look rather upscale and posh, with a bit of
staff now and then both in the house and in the garden. This
country will not change for you, although it will require you
to change for it in order to discover a rewarding place here.
A good way to look at this is that growth and change is the
reason you came. We all could have stayed just the same back
at home and always known what to expect. This is not a place
for people who can't handle surprises or have lost their knack
for improvisation.

For those in the United States with a cynical attitude
toward México, it will not surprise them when I say you will
sometimes pay for more than you get here. There is not the
attitude toward customer service we are used to, and there are
more people here than in the north who believe it their sacred
duty to cheat you. Operate with more care in routine commerce. On the other hand, you will often also get more than
you pay for because so many of the best things here are free.
This is both a song title and a cliché up north, but a reality

down here.

Still, it is possible to live your expat life in an enclave, an English speaking colony like San Miguel, Lake Chapala, or some of the beach communities, and operate so embedded within your peer group that your principal point of contact with México is only the bureaucracy and the weather. But that will not be the real México. I have heard people disparage San Miguel as a kind of Disneyland México, but that is a shallow take on it. The truth is that the real México is all around you in this town and to miss it you would have to actively choose not to see it.

In terms of the contemporary world, this is not only an older country than both the U.S. and Canada, but a far more traditional one. The structure and habits of the ancient indigenous culture have been absorbed into both colonial, and then into modern México, where they may have been renamed and recharacterized, but they were never eradicated or replaced. Witness the names of most of the cities here, for example, our neighbor, Santiago de Querétaro, with a population of one point nine million. These place names are usually comprised of the original pre-Columbian name combined with a saint's name grafted on, often at the front. The significance of this is more than symbolic. It suggests that the entire structure of European culture is overlaid on an indigenous base that continues to grow within its own boundaries, even as it works to maintain its traditional values. Much of it is unconnected to our need to go to Costco or any other big box store. It is what it is, and it will survive us all. Expats will do best by opening their eyes and getting involved. There is much more to it than watching our neighbors dancing around wearing indigenous outfits during fiestas.

People here are accustomed to doing things as they have always done them. In this context, they feel that no explanation for this is required, and to ask for one evokes a reaction of startled surprise. The appropriate English response would be, "Because." Continuity is a self-evident value. There is usually only one way to do things; the way they have always been done. After all, didn't that work before? The world our Mexican neighbor sees is more static than ours. The latest cell phone from Apple may be something of a status symbol, a new toy, but it will never alter the course of day-to-day reality in the way it has always been experienced. Time moves differently in different categories, and the time of technology travels at a different pace than the time of tradition. This is not a distinction we are accustomed to.

Since these systems are not typically negotiable, it works better to learn the customs so that we know what to expect, rather than seek to alter them, which only engenders frustration on both sides.

Recently, for example, we had outages in our Internet service. It would simply go off Sunday afternoons at two P.M. and resume at some unpredictable time on Monday. As for my reaction to this, I will simply say that as a writer, my continued residence in México depends on Internet service. Doing what I do, I couldn't have lived here in 1985.

The first week of this you would accept with an attitude of expectant forbearance. You never know when an event is part of a pattern, or simply random. Later in the second week of this, a pair of service representatives appeared at the door with a new modem to exchange for the old one. Was this because of the outages? They had no idea, there were simply replacing all of them. I was cautiously hopeful. They could not, however, get the new modem to work once connected. Did they stay with it until it did? No. Did they reinstall the old one, which had generally worked, except on Sunday afternoons and evenings and Monday mornings? No. Did they phone the office to set up another service call for us? No. There is a strong work ethic here. People take their jobs quite seriously for the most part and can be relied upon to carry out their task list. The task for these two technicians was to go house to house and exchange the modems. That is what they did. That is also *all* they did, since that was what their task list told them to do. Were they insensitive or uncooperative? No, they were doing their jobs.

The next day I went into the office in person (no service phone number is listed). The service rep was polite as she listened to my problem. I was told it would take twenty-four hours for a technician to appear. It was scheduled for between nine and two the next day, a Friday. At two the next day, when no one had appeared, I flew down to the main office in an artificial state of calm and threw myself on the mercy of a different service representative. I was bringing out a book, I said (this book), and it was critical that I be able to reach people by email throughout the weekend as I finalized the details. Monday was a holiday, the birthday of Benito Juárez, so the cable offices would be closed for three days. I would be frozen in place. The service person went next door to speak with her boss. She returned with his solemn oath that someone would fix my service by the end of that day, Friday. I was not enormously surprised when no one did, but I *had* hit the wall. It was not just that no technician appeared, it was that I was lied to about their imminent arrival, twice. This from a national communications company. In the States we would find this inexplicable, at least when I still lived there.

On Saturday morning at ten I went down to the phone company and signed up for *their* Internet service. I was given a modem and a DVD with installation instructions, and I was back in business by noon. At one o'clock the phone company called me to ask if everything was working to my satisfaction.

On Tuesday I went down to turn in the modem to the old Internet provider. The service woman recognized me, and in surprise, asked me why I was cancelling the service. I won't repeat what I said, but I knew it was what any gringo would say. I felt bad about that, but this experience had struck at the core of my business, and I couldn't take that lightly.

A long story, perhaps, but the detail is revealing about Mexican attitudes and practices in business. You can encounter a large company that does business as if it was operating in the U.S., and with those same standards of customer service, and also one, like our original Internet provider, that operates on fate and good intentions, and does not understand why that isn't good enough for everyone.

My point is that we should strive as residents in this unfamiliar, and very foreign land, to do better than I did with the Internet. One thing we can learn from this frustrating parable is that Mexican customers are often more patient than we are accustomed to be. They clearly have lower expectations, and therefore lower blood pressure. They are also, in a general way more literal-minded than we are. When, as employees, they are told what their job is, that is what they do, and they are rarely inclined to improvise outside the framework of their instructions. This is not a condescending thing to say. It comes from centuries of layered authority, carefully calibrated and jealously guarded. You do only your job, because to improvise is to make decisions outside of your range of authority, and therefore to intrude upon those whose power goes beyond yours. When you think outside the box, your box, you are intruding on someone else's box.

When that first crew left me with no Internet service, a situation that was an outcome of their own actions, they were satisfied that they had done their job. The function of the new modem was not something they had much control over.

This is one of the reasons that fate is so often invoked here as a cause of events. Human causality has a limited range, while fate can explain anything.

So what can we say then, about people who do well in this cultural environment that may seem skewed relative to ours? Is this a place where natural victims manage better than others? No, because they will be just as well misused back in the U.S. or Canada. When I worked on my earlier book about the expat experience in places with no special support group, I asked everyone what they had learned from living in México. In nearly every response the word *patience* appeared in the first sentence of their answer. Patience is the magical lubricant that makes these imperfect interactions survivable. It is what makes the constant disconnect between our culture and theirs manageable. It can sometimes make the near misses close to rewarding. If we do not possess patience, or cannot summon it, it is better to stay home. Come down for two weeks to the beaches in February, but change locations frequently and don't ever buy a house.

My own issue in this situation was that I couldn't manage patience when I was surrounded by deadlines in the midst of what to me was an unnecessary communications breakdown. Since it was connected to my livelihood, I didn't feel I could accept anything that didn't fix the problem. But that was largely a matter of perspective—mine.

So yes, or rather, no, San Miguel is not for everyone. It's not for those who need it to be today on the calendar, or to be cutting edge, because in many areas here it's unclear what year it is. Maybe on a good day it feels like 1985, even when in México City it can look like 2037. Be prepared to allow for these regional differences that go beyond daylight savings time or Mountain, Central, Pacific, or Eastern Time zones. Long before Einstein figured it out, Mexicans knew that time is not absolute, nor is anything else here.

Another point to raise is that as expats we do not own this town. There is a tendency for expats who have been here a long time to pull rank. If I say to someone that I have lived here for seven years, he or she may say with a knowing smile, "I've been here eighteen." The word *novice* is implied by his tone. "You should've seen it in the nineties. It's just not the same anymore now. It's a different kind of people coming in than there used to be." A rueful shake of the head follows.

That's probably true in some ways, but it's also true of the people who came here thirty years ago, who might've wished this guy had ended up in Veracruz instead of San Miguel. Is one of these layered groups superior to another? They may be in their own minds. I think of this attitude as the *Lock the Door After Me* mindset. In other words, I'm here now, I've achieved my goal, so this place may not change any further, and I've a good mind not to let anyone else in, just to keep it the way it was the day I arrived. In a single word, it's called seniority, a concept that has worked with limited success in labor unions, but in few other places.

The reality is that in San Miguel we occupy just one rung on a ladder of evolutionary change. The next rung, when we are gone, will be occupied by expats different from us, people we may not consider worthy of this privilege. In turn, they will look back on us as quaint early settlers, somewhat like pioneers, and wonder how we got by with the limited technology and resources available here. They will probably think our rotary cell phones were made of wood.

One thing I will testify to is that here you can live more in the moment. If you have only six years to live, go ahead and spend them in México. They may not be longer in duration, but they will definitely be more fully and intensely packed. Why give up easily? You can come here either to live or to die, and I can recommend this country in either case. You also can do either one more inexpensively than in the U.S. or Canada. To me, dying in Illinois or Idaho, or Yellow Knife, seems pointless. Better to die in a place that makes a statement on your way out, for example, that you lived each moment to the end, and you damn well *knew* what you were doing when you made that decision. But let go of the reins as you cross the border, and start to loosen up, because close control will evade you here. Accept serendipity as a lifestyle. Some people near the end of their lives seem to have a need to do everything in the same way, every day, even when they're in good health, as if it's only repetition that will sustain them. If that is you, and you cannot change that approach, then San Miguel de Allende will mostly likely not be a good fit for you.

I think that by now I have established that México is not for everyone. You know who you are, or at least you're starting to suspect it. If the need for control is your fundamental style, then stay home and try to make that work. If consumerism is your mantra, then stay home to cultivate that, because we don't think of ourselves that way down here. We don't feel superior because of this, only different. We've chosen another fork in the road, and friends and family relationships matter more. If you are measured by what you own, more than by what you are or would like to do or be, then don't spend the money on a passport. They keep going up in cost all the time, and moving all that stuff down here can cost a bundle.

But if you can still ease yourself gingerly into another culture, like a pool whose water temperature you're not too certain of, if you can try to understand what you're looking at, even when it's something you didn't grow up with, then this may be the right turn for you. The rewards will be worth the efforts you invest to discover them.

CONCLUSION

My research has not been exhaustive, since my approach is usually to try to get inside a phenomenon by talking to people who know about it, who are living it, or by observing it closely myself, rather than by combing statistics and the analyses of outsiders. Clearly, your experience of San Miguel will differ from mine. Yet, I have to conclude that while there is no earthly paradise, it is still amply possible that there are places far better than the one you are planning to leave. This is not to say that it's only a matter of exchanging one set of problems for another, but with a much better climate and a significantly lower cost of living.

Part of the issue is the divergence between what we expect paradise to be and what the destination really is in itself. Whether you are disappointed as the truth unfolds about your new way of life in México will depend on how well you have prepared yourself for the transition. While there is a certain tilted charm in coming down here and buying a house on impulse on the day you were planning to leave, the most successful adaptations are going to be made by those people who have done their homework, and reading this book is one part of that process, but far from the only one.

Be Prepared is not only the Boy Scout motto; it is the best advice for someone who's considering trying out the expatriate experience. Living in a new country is more easily accomplished by the young and flexible than by those of us whose life history has largely been played out somewhere else. Yet, rising to the demands of a new location, culture, and lifestyle is likely to make us both feel and be younger, rather than the opposite. The degree to which we have examined in advance the detail of the situation we're about to enter will partly determine how well it plays out for each of us. That is at the core of my message to the present reader.

I have approached this investigation into the expat life in San Miguel without sentiment. Indeed, my job is always to be a true observer, which in my view, is a high and often challenging task. Like any other country or town I've visited, this place has its warts.

Looking back on what I've written, in some ways I find the DOG LIFE chapter the most moving; an odd choice, perhaps, given some of the others, but it illustrates some harsh but fundamental realities about a country that is simultaneously first, second and third world in its differing elements. In the life of dogs I see implicit parallels to the human condition here. Some get lucky and are born to wealth and privilege, but for most life can be rough and unaccommodating. It can be challenging at every turn. As expats arriving with some resources and life experience, it can also be rewarding and supportive of changes in our thinking and creative lives in ways no other place has ever been.

While I have never shirked from mentioning the negative aspects of living in San Miguel, it may be appropriate to underweight them somewhat against several of the positive ones. Like the issue of avoiding the purchase of a house with most of its windows facing an empty lot, much of the potential risk is easily dodged once it's recognized, but the positive aspects of living here are often huge and lasting, and cannot be found in every other place we might consider. After more than seven years in residence I see no reason to leave. If conditions changed here and I felt I needed to live elsewhere, I would go further into Latin American rather than back to the U.S.

Although the border remains in a stubbornly fixed position, the U.S. itself slips farther away all the time, on its own obscure path, as if retreating from something, and more than one thing, that it once stood for. Is it some kind of unscientific continental drift? Perhaps the border itself, once a thin line, is now growing in width, pushing the two sides further apart every day. Or is the drift mainly one of perspective, of point of view, of orientation—even of relief? Looking around at his or her situation and needs, the reader will decide.

Like others in this story, I find an unusual freedom in México as a whole, and in San Miguel in particular, to both be and do what I want. There is no chapter in this book called freedom, because it is far more than the mere absence of restraint, and therefore hard to define, yet it is the implicit focus of the entire message. Think of it as the subtext of this ongoing story, as indeed it is.

Therefore I will end this book as I ended another book of mine, *A Writer's Notebook*, with the same phrase, a damn good one then, and one that I still live by: Go For It!

RESOURCES

This section is all about lists. What is available here?

ACCESS SAN MIGUEL

The usual place to start for a general search for virtually anything is Access San Miguel. Here is how it describes itself:

Find over 1,880 accurate and useful business and service listings for San Miguel de Allende, Mexico: Phone, address, contact/management, e-mail, web and map position, satellite view and street view. Plus ratings and a place to leave your opinions.

http://accesssanmiguel.com

It's a truly exhaustive list, and I've referred to it several times in the text of this book.

THE CIVIL LIST

A community billboard with about 8,000 members. Useful for staying abreast of activities, events and local concerns.

https://groups.yahoo.com/neo/groups/Civil_SMA/info

CONCERT SERIES
International Chamber Music Festival
www.festivalsanmiguel.com/

International Festival of Jazz & Blues:
www.sanmigueljazz.com.mx/festival_english.html

Opera San Miguel
http://operasanmiguel.org/home.html

Pro Musica of San Miguel de Allende:
www.promusicasma.com/

INFORMATION BILLBOARDS:

Atención, San Miguel's weekly bilingual newspaper.
It comes out on Fridays. The Que Pasa section details upcoming events in every field.
www.sanmiguelevents.com/

RELIGION

An excellent list of religious services can be found at:
http://vivasanmiguel.com/community/churches.htm
Day by day lists of other events and activities are also covered.

SAN MIGUEL MEDICAL RESOURCE DIRECTORY

A comprehensive list of medical practitioners and facilities. Indispensible.
http://www.smahealthinfo.com

SCHOOLS—LANGUAGE
There are several large language schools easily found online, but I want to mention three smaller ones that give a more intimate experience of language study.

Academia Hispano Americana
Mesones #4 415 152 0349
An immersion school with classes in the morning, all taught by native Spanish speakers, with lectures and activities in the afternoon. Tuition is $215 for one week to $650 for four weeks. Will arrange home stay with a Mexican family if desired.

info@ahaspeakspanish.com

http://www.ahaspeakspanish.com

Habla Hispana
Calzada de la Luz 25 415 152 0713
An immersion school with private and small group lessons conducted in Spanish. Each four-week term includes eighty hours of intensive Spanish in the classroom, plus twenty-four hours of cultural extracurricular activities such as Mexican songs, cooking classes, and guided walking tours of San Miguel. Currently tuition is $170 for one week to $560 for four weeks. Homestay with a Mexican family is $26usd/day per person or $21usd/day per person for couples.

info@mexicospanish.com

http://www.mexicospanish.com

Liceo de la Lengua
Callejón del Pueblito #5, between Relox and Hidalgo streets. 415 121 2535

http://liceodelalengua.com

Immersion school with private and small group lessons conducted in Spanish plus field trips, fiestas, and other extracurricular activities. Tuition per week is $55usd-$180usd (one hour to four hours a day) or $200usd-$680usd per month (one hour to four hours a day). Private tutoring $15usd per one-hour session or $70usd-$115usd per week (one hour or two hour sessions).

SCHOOLS—PRIVATE

Jose Vasconselos, a bilingual coed school running pre-school through middle school.

http://jose-vasconcelos.edu.mx/english/index-en.html

Victoria Robbins School, a bilingual school

https://www.facebook.com/pages/Victoria-Robbins-School/170317429745297

Academia Internacional San Miguel de Allende, a recently opened K-12 school with more than 200 students.

www.academysanmiguel.org

SOCIAL AND NEWCOMERS' GROUP

Watch for monthly notices of meetings on the San Miguel Civil list.

BOOKS

I had originally intended to include a chapter titled MANNERS, which matter in México more than they do in the north, and often in different ways. This is not a "melting pot" kind of culture, where elements from societies all over the world have joined over centuries to build a loose and at times unconnected social structure. It is a much more traditional culture formed mainly by the interaction of the related indigenous peoples with their Spanish colonial conquerors. It is less receptive to change than more technology-oriented societies, and therefore more conservative in retaining traditional values and mores.

These manners both supply the framework and

furnish the lubricant for social interaction in México. Their forms vary greatly according to the relationship between the people who are interacting. They underline the differences in social rank, express the nuances of relationships that lie below the surface, and at times they even contradict the overt meaning of the message in a conversation. Because they are so specific to Mexican culture, they are also often invisible to expats, who therefore tend not to learn or try to practice them. And because we often do not practice them, running on a different set we absorbed growing up in Canada or the United States, Mexicans often have the impression that we have no manners ourselves.

I had conducted an interview with a mixed Mexican/Canadian couple that I thought would give a good overview of this issue, and they were very cooperative and enlightening, but I found when I tried to write it that what I mainly had was a list of items that said, "Do this under these circumstances, or don't do that, etc." I began to realize that what I really wanted was a chapter on the Mexican character that, like an umbrella, would include all the nuances of manners and many other things as well.

This was beyond the scope of that chapter, and beyond the scope of this book as well. The subject would require a book on its own, so I abandoned that question for this one. It's also beyond the scope of my grasp of the subject, so I am going to recommend a superb book titled *Mañana Forever*, by Jorge G. Castañeda, Alfred A. Knopf, 2011. In it the author examines the Mexican character in the light of where México stands in the world today.

Another book I highly recommend, although it's not focused on San Miguel, either, is David Lida's *First Stop in the New World*, Riverhead Books, 2008. This portrait of México City is broad enough to illuminate an entire range of Mexican character traits and well worth a read for those interested in understanding this culture.

Last, I strongly recommend *There's a Word for It in Mexico*. This is an older book (1996), by Boyé Lafayette De Mente from NTC Publishing Group, but utterly timeless, and at this writing it's still available on Amazon. It's structured like a cultural dictionary with each Spanish word followed by a brief article about its significance. Highly instructive, and as far as I know, unique.

Please visit the author's website at:
www.sanmiguelallendebooks.com
Twitter: @MEXTEXT
Facebook: https://www.facebook.com/?ref=tn_tnmn